I0478659

Project Fresh Start, The Politics of Prosperity, Part II, with Common Sense
by Anonymous

Introduction

We humbly invite our readers to use Startpage to anonymously search any documented content they doubt.

On 10 January 1776, an English corset-maker by the name of Thomas Paine published an anonymous best-selling revolutionary short simple 48 page pamphlet called '*Common Sense.*'

Paine had the volunteer help of American founding fathers Benjamins Franklin and Rush, polymath authors, diplomat, inventor, Junto founder, physician or scientist.

Common Sense, original title *Plain Truth*, printed 500,000 copies bought by 2.5 million Americans in the colony at the time.

This was the largest per capita sale and circulation of any publication in American history.

Common Sense was bought by one fifth of the American population, circulated widely to coworkers, family, friends and read by many more.

Common Sense was a timely sermon on the power of Liberty.

Liberty was sorely needed by colonials oppressed by the crown, intimidated by force and taxed without representation, with many violations of the sovereign rights of a free people.

Paine anonymously donated the royalties to George Washington's Continental Army for the purchase of mittens to prevent frostbite. We donate them to a modern campaign for freedom.

202 years after Common Sense, we taught a modest evening Stanford Special course called *Mind Money Market* by Academic Senate appointments for five years. MMM was popular because it was practical. What bright, motivated, talented students wanted to know then, as ever, was how to make their family fortune with freedom and responsibility; how to keep it.

Apple, now the largest corporation by stock market capitalization in the world, went public in 1980 during MMM. Apple created more millionaires than any other IPO (Initial Public Offering) up to that time.

This included the record-setting Ford IPO in 1956, which became a powerful rich tax-free foundation after the passing of assembly-line manufacturing pioneer Henry Ford. Ford paid his non-union productive workers twice the prevailing wage from 1914 through the Depression in Dearborn and Detroit. His vision of efficient productivity raised the general standard of living, and created many new Ford customers.

Ford had worked evenings for Edison, who knew 1000 ways not to build a light. Ford learned from daytime entrepreneurial failures with the Quadricycle and Detroit Automobile Company. When Ford unionized with the UAW (United Auto Workers) in 1941, he was already building airplanes and tractors. Ford went from the most stubborn union holdout to the most favorable UAW contract terms. Ford opposed financiers and wars as a terrible waste.

One interesting factoid re life in the fast lane:

Of the 261 Wall Street Firms that took the private $188 Billion (in today's dollars) Ford family business fortune public in 1956 after Henry Ford passed, only 12 exist today.

In 1980, Microsoft (1986), Google (2004) and Facebook (2012) IPOs were yet to come.

One issue Apple millionaires and billionaire venture capitalists had in 1980 was estate and income tax rates up to 70% (28% on long-term Capital Gains).

Tax shelters had high, sometimes retroactive tax law liabilities, little safety or long-term viability, tax recaptures with uneconomic returns.

Many of the MMM Stanford class questions involved death, government and taxes.

Income taxes throughout history ranged from the biblical 10% tithe to 20% tax in ancient Egypt, up to 94% under FDR, prolonging the Great Depression 37 years in real terms.

In fact, FDR proposed a 100 percent top tax rate.

At a time of "grave national danger," Roosevelt told Congress in April 1942:

"No American citizen ought to have a net income, after he has paid his taxes, of more than $25,000 a year."

In early October 1942, FDR issued an Executive Order that limited top corporate salaries to $25,000 after taxes.

That order was repealed by Congress. But by war's end, America's wealthy were paying taxes on income over $200,000 at a 94 percent statutory rate.

Does that sound familiar today?

According to Official Department of Labor BLS (Bureau of Labor Statistics) CPI (Consumer Price Index) numbers revised downward by government many times to diminish COLA (Cost of Living Adjustments) payments for government pensions and social security, $200,000 in 1945 was worth $2,594,488.89 today.

$200,000 today is a lot less than it was in 1945, just $15,411.22 then, according to United States Department of Labor BLS CPI figures.

During and after the years at Stanford and Stanford Capital, aspiring Silicon Valley Millionaires and Billionaires, some with family legacies, asked creative, off the wall, out-of-the-box questions.

One wanted to fund his fortune with a 21% APR (Annual Percentage Rate) credit card because he had no savings.

As Billionaire Sir John Templeton said in Lyford Cay, he saved half of what he earned and never borrowed, which wasn't easy at the start.

As Confucius, Moses, Mohammad, Christ and Ben Franklin knew, money changer usury always eventually compounded out of control. The basis of all wealth is thrift, a moral lesson for success largely forgotten today with fear and greed.

These class and client questions stimulated communication with free market monetarist

Milton Friedman, Fed Chair Alan Greenspan, Economists Michael Boskin and Gary Shilling and libertarian author Thomas Sowell.

In 1963 Milton Friedman and Anna Jacobsen Schwartz finished their lengthy academic study, 'A Monetary History of the United States (1867-1960).' Their work claimed steady monetary policy could have prevented the Great Depression.

In 1980 Milton Friedman and his wife Rose wrote a best-seller, 'Free to Choose.' FTC became a ten-part TV series on many PBS stations used as a fundraiser. Their central idea was that free markets solve more problems and create more prosperity for more members of society more efficiently than any other economic political system.

How far we came since 1980. Then a President espousing free markets was elected to save America from decline with the "Reagan Revolution."

Alan Greenspan is a Juilliard Jazz Clarinet Saxophone player economic consultant (mutual saxophone friend the late Stan Getz), who, before becoming Federal Reserve Governors Chair, advocated gold in his 1966 essay in Ayn Rand's Capitalism, The Unknown Ideal.

Some think Dr Greenspan used the price of gold as an interest rate proxy to contract and expand the nominal money supply to keep it steady in real terms.

From August 1987 to 31 January 2006, 18.5 years, the second longest Fed Governor Chair tenure, Dr Greenspan presided over a generational bull market in Treasury bonds that went from a yield of 10.25% to 4.46% for a total return over four times, and a stock market (Standard & Poor's 500) that went from an October 1987 crash low of 216.45 to a high of 1297.57, for a six-fold return plus dividends, despite decrying *irrational exuberance* in 1996.

Michael Boskin, who shares my daughter's birthday, was a distinguished Stanford Economics Academic Sponsor for MMM. He went on to become Chairman of President HW Bush's Council of Economic Advisers, serve on the Boards of Various multinationals including XOM (Exxon Mobil) and helped save government pensions and Social Security by defining down the CPI (Consumer Price Index) COLA's (Cost of Living Adjustments). Multinationals went overseas for even cheaper manufacturing labour, natural resources and technology transfer.

(Adam Smith held that mercantilist balance of trade concerns and doctrines were absurd, as it all evens out over time with currency fluctuations. The adjustment getting there can be tough for many. Politics is about the majority.)

Dr Boskin has written extensively about tax reform.

Fellow beekeeper Gary Shilling went from a Phi Beta Kappa in Physics at my college to a Stanford PhD in economics, the San Francisco Fed and Exxon's economic department, to founding the Merrill Lynch's Economics department. He left Merrill for Whiteweld after some customers complained to CEO (Chief Executive Officer) Don Regan Dr Shilling was too bearish in 1973 (the proper time to be bearish, as the Dow (Dow Jones Industrials) fell almost in half from 1051.70 to 577.60 in two years.)

Merrill acquired Whiteweld and Dr Shilling, who may have been an architect for Merrill's 1981 Dawn of a New Bull Market, when Treasury Bonds were yielding 14% and the Dow was under 1000.

Lots of clients, family and friends were grateful for his advocacy of long-term positions in bonds.

One told me when she was a little girl, she did not ask her Greenwich, CT grandfather for dolls or ponies, but bonds and stocks.

Dr Shilling went on to advise presidential candidates about economic disinflation and deflation, a significant concept for those assuming eternal inflation. At some point, debt compounds to the point it is no longer serviceable and collapses.

Yale economist Irving Fisher, whom Nobel Economic Laureates Milton Friedman and James Tobin called the greatest American economist, delivered a 17 October 1929 Harvard Economic Society speech claiming the stock market was on a permanently high plateau.

A few years later he described debt default deflation.

Bullish investment booms and bubbles turn into bearish contractionary busts, even debt Sabbaticals and Jubilee forgiveness (named after the 7-year and 50-year debt cycles in the Mosaic Old Testament Exodus, Leviticus and Numbers.) Employment contracts, long-term bonds, credit cycles, mortgages and property leases still reflect this today.

Thomas Sowell is a prolific free market author and Rose and Milton Friedman Senior Fellow at the Hoover Institution. Dr Sowell was a high school dropout from Harlem who served in the Marine Corps during the Korean War and returned to Harvard, Columbia and Chicago for a doctorate in economics. He is the author of more than 30 books. A National Humanities Medal winner, he advocates laissez-faire economics and writes from a conservative and libertarian perspective.

The Hoover Institution Tower houses Stanford Mining Engineer President Hoover's Library of War, Revolution and Peace.

(Speaking of War, I learned from the All Soul's Diplomatic Divided Nations Seminar organized by Chichele Professor of the History of War and Fellow, All Souls College, co-director All Souls Foreign Policy Studies Programme, Professor Robert O'Neill.)

(Four favourite liberating lifetime political books were Bakeless' '*Turncoats, Traitors and Heroes: Espionage in the American Revolution*,' Dostoyevsky's '*The Possessed (Demons/Devils*),' Billington's '*Fire in the Minds of Men: Origins of the Revolutionary Faith*' and Baran and Sweezy's '*Monopoly Capital: An Essay on the American Economic and Social Order*.')

Stanford Hoover Tower also houses a 48 bell carillon. (The largest bell is 2.5 tons.)

Hoover Tower is where Soviet gulag survivor and author Aleksandr Solzhenitsyn lived on the 11th floor for a time, with a view of San Francisco from Palo Alto on clear days.

Many of my Stanford students were inspired to write impassioned free market papers advocating limits to the growth and scope of big government, lower government borrowing, less red tape, less spending and lower taxes to enhance personal future productivity, peace and prosperity as they started ventures of their own, recreating the golden age of the individual entrepreneur with the "*Less government is more prosperity*" approach.

A number of bright top-tier Stanford athletes enjoyed the MMM course as a guideline for future rational financial decisions. One who started a student mattress company wrote the popular '*Student Entrepreneur's Handbook*.' Brett Kingstone sold quite a few copies. Some are occasionally still available on Amazon.

Another, Heidi Roizen, daughter of an inventor, Stanford Crimson editor, wrote her paper on Housing Options, started a word processing company, T Square, with her brother, befriended Bill and Melinda Gates, sat on the Board of Pacific Options Exchange and became a Venture Capitalist with DFJ, backing more than 400 companies since 1985. Some students served faithfully, humbly and industriously as Research and Teaching Assistants. They helped lost students and scored the student portfolios for prizes. They went on to run the Blyth Student Investment fund I advised. They worked on the *Innovest* software project with a donation from Apple. They started their own ventures or went back home to run or start billion dollar family enterprises around the world.

Many quoted Stanford alumnus Compaq Computer Lotus 123 Spreadsheet founder, venture capitalist Ben Rosen, who said, "*Serious problems in America began when the number of US law school graduates exceeded the number of US engineer graduates.*"

Many foreign US-educated engineers went back home to transfer American intellectual property and practical prowess to their home countries.

When I married to start a family, I stopped teaching and went back to focus on building family assets like a home and retirement.

I did a private equity placement with a Nobel Laureate biotech company and funded a medical device company acquired and taken private for $11.4 Billion. I received half a finder's fee but not stock, due to a misunderstanding. Three of my life lessons were:

A) We cannot out-give Creator,
B) The law of gratitude always attracts more,
C) We are always compensated for our good work, sometimes in mysterious ways.

I was asked by the Stanford Alumni Office to write a Portable Stanford Reader based on the extensive Mind Money Market syllabus after five years. I was too busy earning a living to do it then. It may be a forthcoming publishing project as I occasionally miss The Farm at The Lake.

I had been a coin collector with help from grandparents since Second grade. In those days, a silver certificate paper dollar meant you could exchange it at the bank for a more valuable silver dollar. This amateur arbitrage illustrated Sir Thomas Gresham's Law that "Bad money drives out good."

(Sir Isaac Newton proved Gresham's Law as Master of the Mint with an overvalued gold:silver ratio that caused silver hoarding. While the gold:silver ratio is currently 59, it was fixed at 15 by our forefathers with the Coinage Act of 1792 after Conquistadore stolen New World Silver, with the Spanish Silver Dollar Piece of Eight US legal tender from 1497 to 1857 with the Coinage Act of 1857, a defacto world currency. Before Spain invaded the America's for gold, jewels and silver, silver was as scarce as 10:1 gold:silver during Biblical times.

Copernicus the astronomer, Bishop Oresme, Al Maqrizi, Artistotle and Aristophanes in *The Frogs* discussed Gresham's Law and monetary inflation as early as the Fifth Century BCE.)

I pulled ten weeds for a penny as a child to earn money from my Swiss engineer textile mill grandfather on his Jersey Shore Island property to fund a summer trip to the National Boy Scout Jamboree in Valley Forge. There were a lot of weeds, so he paid the overage in silver dollars, which my practical electrical engineer Navy Officer Manufacturer's Rep Dad exchanged for paper dollars, keeping the silver in the safe per Gresham's Law.

I much later met Burt Blumert, who knew Ron Paul from the Air Force, founded a coin company and was Dr Paul's first Presidential Campaign Adviser. I bought junk silver bags at a discount from Burt until I realized legal tender bullion American Silver Eagles from the US Mint dealer network at a premium, guaranteed by the Secret Service with legal and tax advantages, held liquidity, recognition and value better.

Burt began inviting me to Libertarian Conferences in the 1970s.

I sat at the feet of entertaining insightful Austrian Economist Libertarian Murray Rothbard, a doctoral economics classmate of Alan Greenspan's, and various Paleo-conservatives, passionate classical liberal advocates for the benefits and virtues of freedom and responsibility.

I sophomorically challenged my red-bearded MIT PhD college Economics Professor Ralph Beals, consultant to the Indonesia economic miracle, acting Dean of Faculty and President of the college, re not teaching credit cycle economics in his banking course. Then he sent his syllabus including the (then unpopular) Austrian Economists. I was perhaps distracted at the time by a successful 1970 Cambodia Bombing Moratorium Congressional campaign for Father Drinan, the first US Rep to oppose the war in Vietnam.

Dominant government economics then as now were the neo-Keynesian pseudo religion of something for everyone for nothing inflationary tax theft from the disappearing Middle Class.

Keynesians believed governments could borrow, inflate, spend and tax their way to the appearance of prosperity for at least a special few apparatchiks. Neo-Keynesians believed governments should manage the (mixed) economy for the many in a modern western version of the same central planning that failed economies, futures, peace and people in Cuba, Cyprus, North Korea, Red China, the Soviet Union, Vietnam and Yugoslavia.

If there is one lesson of history, it is that centrally planned and controlled economies fail, from Gibbon's Rise and Decline of Rome to the Black Swan Economic Fail Fall books by Roubini, economic collapse blog posts, youtubes and Zero Hedge today. (Look them up on Startpage.)

Man's creative spirit cannot be caged in a computer or tethered to a GPS (Global Positioning System) car or cell phone.

From 1948 to 1989, despite plenty of evidence to the contrary, the widely-used neo-Keynesian Samuelson Economics academic text claimed the socialist central command mixed economy was superior to the competitive free market and the Soviet economy would eclipse the American economy by 1990. In 1989 the Berlin Wall fell.

This confirmed the widely-held opinion by many business people that academics may be the last to know.

Predictions, particularly concerning the future, are problematic.

Now, as the Red China economy contracts with false statistics and fiat inflation, some still claim China will surpass America by 2017.

This is possible if the American government deficit takeover of the private sector with compulsory healthcare, higher taxes, mandatory military adventurism, more fiat funny money and more red tape, continues to expand.

Central planning, foreign adventurism and imperialism failed throughout history and the world. Ask Alexander, Caesar, Genghis, Hirohito, Hitler, Kaiser, Mao, Mussolini, Napoleon, Ottoman, Stalin et al.

Ironically, after the fall of the Berlin Wall, collapse of the Soviet empire and August putsch of reformer Mikhail Gorbochev in 1991, while on Oxford sabbatical touring Czechoslovakia for export ideas, followed by lawless mafiya and the 1998 Russian Financial Crisis, Vladimir Putin doubled Russian Federation government revenues with a reduced 13% individual and 24% corporate flat tax that cut Russian debt to 8% of the economy and made Russia's trade surplus number three in the world now. This compares to the current US government debt at 106% of the economy, with the largest budget and trade deficits in the world and 20 new or higher taxes up to 43.4% on income.

Academic economists used to say we owed the debt to ourselves, so it did not matter. I tried that with the bank and they did not agree.

China, India and Russia are meanwhile making rapid advances in military technology with their newfound economic strength.

One of the fastest growing and most productive economies in the world now has a 10% flat tax.

Meanwhile, US congressional and government committee economic advisers raised taxes and lowered productivity with their red tape and lack of criminal enforcement on Wall Street for campaign bundlers. In real terms, our economy is currently contracting at a -2% rate. No wonder no jobs.

A camel is a horse designed by a committee.

The academic hearsay popular rumour shibboleths that Keynesian economics and World War II got the US out of the Great Depression with borrow, spend and tax strong arm government economics were simply not true. They are a variation of an economic sophism best described by Bastiat as *the Broken Window Fallacy* (Breaking things and killing people does not really increase life, liberty, peace or prosperity, it just transfers wealth.)

America did not have the same war damage from World War II as Africa, Asia, Australia and

Europe, so we held most of their copper, gold and silver money for safekeeping. Now they want it back and we told Germany and the Netherlands to wait up to seven years..

Economic realities changed while a lot of fat cat economists and politicians were dozing, assuming like Buzz Lightyear, their linear economic extrapolations would hold to infinity and beyond.

First Baron Lord Keynes, Kings College Cambridge Bursar and Mathematician turned Government economist, first lost his fortune in Foreign Exchange, using a macro top-down theoretical investment approach favoured by central planners and investment committees.

Then he successfully managed his college endowment and an insurance company portfolio using bottom-up contrary opinion practical value investing from 1924 to 1946, during the Great Depression and World War II.

Keynes outperformed the UK market 8% a year on a risk-adjusted basis, This was no small feat, since most money managers failed to match the declining markets then, let alone outperform with a positive Alpha, excess return.

(It might be worth discussing compounding and the law of numbers. Many Wall Street firms like to dazzle monopoly media with average performance numbers derived by dividing the current % change of an investment by the number of years, which usually gives a larger number than CAGR (Compound Annual Growth Rate).

For example 8% a year higher than the market sounds like a modestly nice higher return compared to a Dow that went from 90 in 1924 to 212 in 1946, for a 135% change divided by 22 years, or 6% a year.

When we use the CAGR Chimp Calculator on the internet, we see that 6% a year from 1924 to 1946 takes the 90 Dow to 324, not 212.

14% a year CAGR from 1924 to 1946 takes the 90 Dow to a whopping 1607.

Thus we see that compounding and consistency are key.

The same mathematic principle works with seemingly small amounts of debt, inflation or interest.

The reportedly low rate of inflation now, 2%, means prices double in 36 years by the *Rule of 72.* 72/2% = 36 years does not set off many alarms. But the current real 1980 methodology inflation rate of 8% CAGR means prices go up almost 16 times in 36 years.

And a student coming out of school with a $100,000 student loan debt compounding at 6.8% means in 36 years that loan will cost over a million dollars, even if partly subsidized by taxpayers.)

Keynes not only believed in balanced budgets.

He also said:

A) *Logic, like lyrical poetry, is no employment for the middle-aged*

B) *Economics is a very dangerous science*

C) *This long run is a misleading guide to current affairs. In the long run we are all dead. Economists set themselves too easy, too useless a task if in tempestuous seasons they can only tell us that when the storm is past, the ocean is flat again*

D) *Lenin declared the best way to destroy the capitalist system was to debauch the currency. By a continuing process of inflation, governments confiscate, secretly and unobserved, an important part of the wealth of their citizens. By this method they not only confiscate, but confiscate arbitrarily; and, while the process impoverishes many, it actually enriches some*

E) *professional investment may be likened to those newspaper competitions in which the competitors have to pick out the six prettiest faces from a hundred photographs, the prize being awarded to the competitor whose choice most nearly corresponds to the average preferences of the competitors as a whole*

F) *Worldly wisdom teaches that it is better for reputation to fail conventionally than to succeed unconventionally*

G) *Americans are apt to be unduly interested in discovering what average opinion believes average opinion to be; and this national weakness finds its nemesis in the stock market*

H) *Successful investing is anticipating the anticipations of others*

I) *The introduction of a Government transfer tax on all transactions might prove the most serviceable reform available, with a view to mitigating the predominance of speculation in the United States (The Tobin Automatic Payment Transaction Tax)*

J) *You can't push on a string*

K) *Markets can remain irrational longer than we can remain solvent*

L) *If farming were organised like the stock market, a farmer would sell his farm in the morning when it was raining, only to buy it back in the afternoon when the sun came out*

M*) I work for a Government I despise, for ends I think criminal*

N) *All political parties alike have their origins in past ideas and not in new ideas — and none more conspicuously so than the Marxists*

Of Keynesianism and Neo-Keynesianism, Cato Senior Fellow, George Mason Professor and Nobel Laureate in Economics for Public Choice Theory, James Buchanan, wrote:

" *Why does Camelot lie in ruins? Intellectual error of monumental proportion has been made, and not exclusively by the politicians. Error also lies squarely with the economists. The "academic scribbler" who must bear substantial responsibility is Lord Keynes...* "

To be fair to Baron Lord Keynes, he advocated balanced government budgets overall, with government saving during the good years and spending during the bad years, like Joseph and the Pharaoh in Genesis.

That did not happen, or we would not be reading *'Crisis Economics: A Crash Course in the Future of Finance, 'How Markets Fail: The Logic of Economic Calamities'* or *Fresh Start: PoP2 (Politics of Prosperity, Part II)* in 2013 after POP(I) in 1994.

Would that more political government economists practiced economy, with a 16.9 Trillion dollar Treasury Debt and 125 Trillion dollars in unfunded government mandate liabilities 8 times the size of this mixed (up) economy, with 28.4% of Americans defacto unemployed. Perhaps large numbers provide a seductive sense of omnipotence to some.

As I reviewed the classical ideas of the Worldly Philosophers from Thales to Aristotle to Bentham to Fisher to Hayek to Hume to Locke to Marx to Newton to Ricardo, to Rothschilds and Rockefellers, to Smith to Schumpeter, Von Mises and others, to write POP(I), friends urged a run for office in 1994 to help stem the tide of an 85-year trend toward the failing big government welfare state.

President Reagan, on whose Task Force I served, casual friends US Rep Jack Kemp and Steve Forbes, Art Laffer, Paul Craig Roberts and Larry Kudlow, briefly reversed the American loss of economic freedom with their Free Market Libertarian Revolution Supply Side ideas that cut red tape and taxes.

The Reagan Administration reduced the Federal Register of regulations from 87,000 pages to 47,000 pages for regulatory reform.

Taxes were reduced from 70% to 28%.

Those two changes took the Misery Index, inflation plus unemployment, from Carter's 21.78 to Reagan's 7.70.

(The current President's official misery index ranged from 7.30 in July 2009 to 12.97 in September 2011.

The real misery index is currently closer to 8% inflation plus 28% unemployment, equals a record 36%, which monopoly media avoid mentioning at all costs if they want White House access.)

Today we must go on the internet carefully to document undisclosed facts and uncover truth.

One day soon this disruptive liberating DARPA internet invention may be selectively or totally shut down for "domestic security" with cyberkill powers issued by a complicit Congress.

Thus this publication is published in print as well as internet Kindle Nook form to share.

A very congenially devastating President Reagan (" *There you go again*") wrote many of his freedom-based economic speeches along with Peggy Noonan. He was one of four presidents who were Business or Economics Majors. Reagan was a dual Economics and Sociology Major.

Reagan had an instinct for memorable Hollywood political one-liners, from "*Honey, I forgot to duck*" when he was shot 63 days into his first term, lost half his blood with a Blood Pressure of 60, from an unexploded Devastator bullet that lodged near his heart and required 105 minutes of open thoracic surgery at the age of 70, to " *Tear down this Wall*" to his second term campaign theme," *Morning in America*."

We must recall that he was so unpopular with 18% mortgage rates that he almost did not run again, but *stayed the course* as Cal Coolidge (see below) and Joan Quigley advised.

Ronnie Raygun, as some called him for his DARPA Star Wars research and military program of recovery, got along well with all of Congress. When he returned from being shot, he told Congress "*I should be applauding you for your teamwork while I was gone*." This is why Congress named an airport for him and gave him a forever stamp.

Reagan joked, laughed and got much of the job done with Irish family tree Bill Casey, head of the CIA (Central Intelligence Agency), Treasury Secretary Don Regan, CEO (Chief Executive Officer) of Merrill Lynch and Tip O'Neill,

Speaker of the House and other members of Congress from both parties.

Maybe it was Reagan's considerable experience in media for WHO Radio as a Cubs announcer, the General Electric Theater on TV and Warner Brothers Studio, as the Democrat President of the Screen Actors Guild who opposed nuclear weapons.

With a modest weekly WOAK FM radio show on current events and various media appearances on special topics, I and many others on both sides of the aisle were drawn toward Reagan's clear, effective and simple presentations of constructive libertarian practical political ideas.

Reagan was twice defeated running for President.

Destined to become the oldest serving president (77), he remarked in the Presidential Debates, "I am not going to make age an issue of this campaign. I am not going to exploit, for political purposes, my opponent's youth and inexperience."

This generated applause and laughter from the national audience. Mondale (who was 56 at the time), said years later in an interview that he knew at that moment he had lost the 1984 election.

President Reagan also said he did not leave the Democratic Party, it left him. As a former registered Democrat and Republican who worked for significant candidates to change the course of economic government political history, now a small business free market Libertarian, I can relate to both parties that way.

Hollywood partisans in '*The Butler*' did their best to savage the Reagans, as was done to his political soulmate, Prime Minister Maggie Thatcher, in '*The Iron Lady*.' The economies of America and UK have not been the same since either national leader was on the world stage.

Only a few presidents had formal business or economics experience.

George Washington, besides being a surveyor and General, was the largest distiller in the colonies. He warned America to beware of [drunken] entangling foreign alliances.

Silent Cal Coolidge, president of my college before President of the USA, famously proclaimed, " *The business of America is business.*"

He also said in a prosperous time when character counted:

A) *Industry, thrift and self-control are not sought because they create wealth, but because they create character.*

B) *Those who trust to chance must abide by the results of chance.*

C) *Ultimately property rights and personal rights are the same thing.*

D) *Economy is the method by which we prepare today to afford the improvements of tomorrow.*

E) *Civilization and profit go hand in hand.*

F) *No enterprise can exist for itself alone. It ministers to some great need, it performs some great service, not for itself, but for others; or failing therein, it ceases to be profitable and ceases to exist.*

G) *The man who builds a factory builds a temple, that the man who works there worships there, and to each is due, not scorn and blame, but reverence and praise.*

H) *I sometimes wish that people would put a little more emphasis upon the observance of the law than they do upon its enforcement.*

I) *Don't expect to build up the weak by pulling down the strong.*

J) *Collecting more taxes than is absolutely necessary is legalized robbery.*

K) *There is no dignity quite so impressive, and no one independence quite so important, as living within your means.*

L) *To live under the American Constitution is the greatest political privilege that was ever accorded to the human race.*

M) *The government of the United States is a device for maintaining in perpetuity the rights of the people, with the ultimate extinction of all privileged classes.*

N) *No nation ever had an army large enough to guarantee it against attack in time of peace, or ensure it of victory in time of war.*

O) *All growth depends upon activity. There is no development physically or intellectually without effort, and effort means work.*

P) *Knowledge comes, but wisdom lingers. It may not be difficult to store up in the mind a vast quantity of facts within a comparatively short time, but the ability to form judgments requires the severe discipline of hard work and the tempering heat of experience and maturity.*

Q) *We do not need more intellectual power, we need more spiritual power. We do not need more of the things that are seen, we need more of the things that are unseen.*

R) *We need more of the Office Desk and less of the Show Window in politics. Let men in office substitute the midnight oil for the limelight.*

S) *It takes a great man to be a good listener.*

T) *You can't know too much, but you can say too much.*

U) *No person was ever honored for what he received. Honor has been the reward for what he gave.*

V) *Perhaps one of the most important accomplishments of my administration has been minding my own business.*

W) *Duty is not collective; it is personal.*

X) *They criticize me for harping on the obvious; if all the folks in the United States would do the few simple things they know they ought to do, most of our big problems would take care of themselves.*

Y) *I have found it advisable not to give too much heed to what people say when I am trying to accomplish something of consequence. Invariably they proclaim it can't be done. I deem that the very best time to make the effort.*

Z) *"Nothing in this world can take the place of persistence. Talent will not; nothing is more common than unsuccessful people with talent. Genius will not; unrewarded genius is almost a proverb. Education will not; the world is full of educated failures. Persistence and determination alone are omnipotent."*

Writer Dorothy Parker, seated next to Silent Cal at a Washington DC (District of Columbia) dinner, said to him:

"Mr. Coolidge, I've made a bet against a fellow who said it was impossible to get more than two words out of you."

His famous reply: *"You lose."*

JFK (John Fitzgerald Kennedy) enrolled and actually audited Stanford Business School in 1940 after he was accepted in 1935 at the London School of Economics, but too ill to attend.

HW Bush was Phi Beta Kappa in Economics at Yale in three years after he was the youngest pilot in WWII.

W Bush graduated from Harvard Business School.

In contrast to the widespread lack of economic experience or training in most US Presidents, Courts or Congresses, Premier, President and

KGB officer Vladimir Putin earned a 1997 PhD from St Petersburg Mining Institute in " *The Strategic Planning of Regional Resources Under the Formation of Market Relations*."

His work was said by some to have been partly plagiarized from the 1978 management text "*Strategic Planning and Policy*," by University of Pittsburgh professors William R. King and David I. Cleland.)

At least someone now uses American can-do know-how political pragmatism for political prosperity.

Under President Reagan and Vice President Bush, the USA enjoyed the highest economic growth (8+% GDP in 1984) and job creation (16+ Million jobs in 8 years) since 1965, despite monopoly media political ridicule and media tirades of Supply Side Economics as " *trickle down economics*," comparing political policies to bathroom behaviour.

Reagan's job creation was second only to the Clintons' New Democrat Leadership Council 8 years.

Clinton tax cuts and welfare work reform were implemented by the first GOP Congress elected in 1994 since 1947, some 47 years, led by Speaker of the House Newt Gingrich and the Contract with America. I worked with Newt in 1994 on regular GOPAC conference calls, then published House Ways and Means Committee testimony on replacing the income tax for economic growth.

Reagan mixed-laissez faire libertarian neoKeynesian supply side policies created a combined prosperity index of growth and jobs that rivaled Silent Cal Coolidge during the Roaring Twenties.

Unfortunately, both Administrations ignored Austrian credit-cycle Economics and embarked on bubble debt-financed spending sprees that led to major economic dislocations and wars thereafter.

The last two war presidents' political policies of higher borrowing, more spending, more red tape and more taxes with OCare in fact created paltry job growth ranging from W's 0% to O's 0.23%.

Millions of hard-working Americans were forced to join the military and go on food stamps to survive.

Let's repeat that for full comprehension:

The last two American Presidents had 0% and 0.23% job growth for the last 13 years, the politics of poverty.

We the People now suffer contracting real economies and living standards for all Americans.

Half of American households earn less than $53,000.

We the People suffer defacto unemployment at 28% according to Center of Working-Class Studies at Youngstown State University.

We the People suffer a real cost of living recently ranging from 6% to 13% according to John William' Shadowstats, under the current President, a Constitutional Law Professor who describes our Constitution as a living document, not a government iron-clad oath public service contract.

To clearly document the obvious connection between prosperity and taxes:

Calvin Coolidge cut taxes from 56% to 24%
JFK and LBJ cut taxes from 91% to 70%
Ronald Reagan cut taxes from to 69% to 28%

All unleashed record economic growth and employment while they were President.

FDR raised taxes from 63% to 94% after failing to get his 100% tax on incomes over $25,000.
HW Bush raised taxes from 28% to 39.6%.
O raised taxes from 35% to 43.4% so far.

All these Presidents suffered real recessions, what used to be called Depressions.

A recession is when your neighbour is out of work. A depression is when you and your wife are out of work.

There are 20 new OCare taxes working their way into contracting our economy after the W Bush tax cuts were ended by the current administration.

Apologists for big government are pointing out the brief drop in the budget deficit after complaining the miniscule sequester would wreak havoc. Closing White House tours and near space impact object monitors were blamed on sequester, while golf and White House vacations continue with 6 hours a round at taxpayer expense since the current president was a state senator.

OCare is costing money and full time jobs before it is fully implemented.

Some private insurance premiums doubled. Estimates of budget savings before OCare passed, changed to budget losses just after OCare passed. The CBO (Congressional Budget

Office) now estimates that OCare will cost $1.165 trillion more than originally estimated:

A) OCare leaves 30 million people still uninsured.
B) OCare leaves 43% of them unaware they face up to $4700 fines.
C) OCare has 60% of doctors now planning to leave medicine.
D) OCare has Congress, special interests and unions that backed and passed OCare now seeking exemptions or subsidies from it or OCare taxes on their Cadillac Healthcare Plans.
E) OCare, guess who pays the bill?
F) OCare, the 63.4% of Americans still working foot the bill.
G) When they retire, OCare is game over without serious political economic reform.

Fantasy focus group media sound bites from teleprompter readers with enthusiasm, but no practical business experience, all sound good until the bill comes due.

The trouble with socialism, Prime Minister Maggie Thatcher observed, is that it runs out of OPM (Other People's Money).

The record is clear for all to see.

Higher taxes with more debts, red tape and government spending, all slow growth and jobs.

Less government, with lower taxes, less red tape and less spending, all create better growth and jobs.

How did America ever become the largest economy in the world with the highest living standard?

Hint:
it wasn't government abandoning our Constitutional freedoms, borrowing more than we have, legislating red tape, judging for special interests, picking winners, spending our way to war and welfare with higher taxes.

So why don't most politicians just admit the truth, instead of employing empty class warfare rhetoric re how they "*help*" the middle class, with (minimum wage unproductive government jobs), "*shared sacrifice taxes*" and "*taxing the rich,*" while taking millions and billions in payoffs from special interests and their lobbyists to actually hobble and tax the middle class out of existence?

The **Middle Class Working Families Task Force** (MCWFTF) is a United States Federal Government initiative, established in 2009 via presidential memorandum to restore the backbone and prosperity of America. Instead, the current administration and Congress added 20 new OCare taxes and 16,000 new IRS (Internal Revenue Service) agents to the backs of hard-working Americans, with subsidies at taxpayer expense for those who do not work.

The irony is that not only did the IRS practice partisan politics under colour of authority, they also have a Cadillac Health Care plan that is tax penalized under OCare.

Circus sideshow promotor PT Barnum said, *there's a sucker born every minute.*

American voters are no longer suckers.

American voters withdrew from the political process in droves, what Confucius, Lao Tzu, Plato, Plotinus, the Crusades, Ibn Khaldun, the Inquisition, Witch hunts, Comte, Hegel, Pinel, Spencer, Marx, Merton, C Wright Mills, Durkheim, Kierkegaard, Heidegger, Weber, Levi-Strauss, Fromm, the Lost Generation, Marshall McLuhan and other students of society called *alienation.*

The worse the economy gets, the fewer votes.

With a modicum of inspiration, this could be the exact opposite, with more people voting for constructive Constitutional government and a better economy with sound money.

The facts are that taxes on the very rich fell from 60% in 1945 to 19% in 2005.

The baby boomer prospered until deliberate government policy by 1% special interests undermined the American standard of living and way of life by shipping jobs overseas and importing illegal minimum wage labour.

Taxes recently rose under the current Administration, Congress and Courts.

The ultra-rich have long-had their tax-free foundations and tax gimmicks.

In 1994 we published simple time-honoured economic political prosperity solutions found in our Declaration of Independence, United States Constitution and Bill of Rights, with our Politics of Prosperity.

These simple ideas still carry profound protections for life, liberty and the pursuit of happiness for all, unless you were an Indentured servant, Indian or Slave.

Full disclosure: I tan red. I am part Delaware Indian, Turtle Clan, who met William Penn's Quakers in 1681 and signed a 70 year land and peace treaty in 1683 under an elm tree in what is now Penn Treaty Park in Philadelphia next to the Delaware River:

Delaware Indians sign Treaty of Penn
with Benjamin West, a painting

Delaware Turtle Clan Chief Tammanend was the inspiration for Tammany Societies, Benjamin Franklin and George Washington. The Delaware were part of the Iroquois Confederation of Nations with their Constitution well before the US Constitution. Delaware Indians signed the first Treaty with the US on 17 September 1778, a fact recognized by Concurrent Resolution 331 on 4 October 1988 in the Second Session of Congress.

A later Delaware Turtle Clan chief ancestor converted to Christianity with the Jan Hus Moravian Missionaries. They were not scalped, but saved by the Delaware Turtle Clan, who converted to Christianity when they saw their peace.

The POP (Politics of Prosperity) result in 1994 was a 100+ page manifesto for the Politics of Prosperity.

We ran ads in *Investor's Business Daily* and took POP on the talking circuit to test the waters for Congress.

We were in a big government district with two to one D:R registration and a long-term incumbent Congressman Professor charged with embezzling significant university student exchange funds. He was forced to return them by a US Congressman after lengthy investigation. The Congressman was later assassinated at Jonestown and his aide, who was shot and survived, now holds the seat.

Monopoly media covered up the embezzlement, as we learned from investigative media reporters whose stories were spiked by editors following orders. Only alternative media carried the story.

The cover-up made the politician easier to control by hidden money special interests that Woodrow Wilson, a Princeton Professor, New Jersey Governor and President, attacked, decried and lambasted to win election as President with classic Br'er Rabbit Briar Patch bait and switch strategy.

In 1913 Wilson published a campaign book, ' *The New Freedom: A Call for the Emancipation of the Generous Energies of a People.*"

In the book he wrote:

"*Since I entered politics, I have chiefly had men's views confided to me privately. Some of the biggest men in the United States, in the field of commerce and manufacture, are afraid of somebody, are afraid of something. They know that there is a power somewhere so organized, so subtle, so watchful, so interlocked, so complete, so pervasive, that they had better not speak above their breath when they speak in condemnation of it.*"

and

"*A great industrial nation is controlled by its system of credit. Our system of credit is privately concentrated. The growth of the nation, therefore, and all our activities are in the hands of a few men ... [W]e have come to be one of the worst ruled, one of the most completely controlled and dominated, governments in the civilized world—no longer a government by free opinion, no longer a government by conviction and the vote of the majority, but a government by the opinion and the duress of small groups of dominant men.*"

Once elected, Wilson signed the very Federal Reserve and IRS Acts that gave the hidden money trust usury control over the Constitutional gold and silver sovereign money power of *We the people*, relegating Congress an illusory supervisory role.

The Fed was presented as a currency reform law to aid business and end all crashes and panics:

DECEMBER 24, 1913-SIXTEEN PAGES. PRICE TWO CENTS

PRESIDENT'S SIGNATURE ENACTS CURRENCY LAW

Wilson Declares It the First of Series of Constructive Acts to Aid Business.

Makes Speech to Group of Democratic Leaders.

Conference Report Adopted in Senate by Vote of 43 to 25.

Banks All Over the Country Hasten to Enter Federal Reserve System.

Gov-Elect Walsh Calls Passage of Bill A Fine Christmas Present.

PRESIDENT WOODROW WILSON.

WILSON SEES DAWN OF NEW ERA IN BUSINESS

Aims to Make Prosperity Free to Have Unimpeded Momentum.

HOME VIEWS OF CURRENCY ACT

"A Christmas present to the people of the country," is the name Gov-Elect David I. Walsh gives to the Currency act.

"I think," he said last night, "that President Wilson and the National Congress are to be congratulated upon the enactment of the Currency bill.

"The purpose of the act is one

FOUR PENS USED BY PRESIDENT

WASHINGTON, Dec 23—President Wilson signed the Glass-Owen Currency bill at 6:01 o'clock tonight in the presence of members of his Cabinet, the Congressional Committee on Banking and Currency and Democratic leaders in Congress generally.

With a few strokes of the pen, the President converted into law

Federal Reserve

The crashes and panics continued, notably 1929.

For this unconstitutional sellout (there was deliberately no Central Bank in our US Constitution), Wilson received the highest honours from the hidden money trust, his face on the $100,000 gold certificate issued, ironically, after gold was outlawed for American citizens, but not the money trust:

Series 1934 $100,000 bill, obverse

Series 1934 $100,000 bill, reverse

After promising not to, during his presidential campaign, Wilson took America into World War I for money trust war profits on both sides. He negotiated steep Versailles German War Reparations for the banks that led to German hyperinflation, economic collapse and World War II.

Wilson lay in the Lincoln Bed in 1919 after suffering a disabling stroke on his left side that left him blind in one eye and paralyzed. His chief of staff and wife secretly ran America for 17 months until his term was over, with photo ops of him signing bills with his good arm.

Wilson was reported by numerous documented sources to have said of the Federal Reserve, which is neither Federal nor a real money Reserve:

"*I am a most unhappy man. I have unwittingly ruined my country.*"

Startpage search Federal Reserve or Fort Knox Gold Gone.

Fort Knox gold has not been thoroughly audited for gold assay since Ike was president in 1953 sixty years ago.

98% of Federal Reserve Deep storage gold belongs to foreign central banks.

The current Fed Chair told US Representative Ron Paul that gold (silver) are not money, despite our US Constitution declaring in Article I, Section 10:

No State shall enter into any Treaty, Alliance, or Confederation; grant Letters of Marque and Reprisal; coin Money; emit Bills of Credit; make any Thing but gold and silver Coin a Tender in Payment of Debts; pass any Bill of Attainder, ex post facto Law, or Law impairing the Obligation of Contracts, or grant any Title of Nobility.

Focused, highlighted and repeated for emphasis:

No State shall...make any Thing but gold and silver Coin a Tender in Payment of Debts.

This may seem inconsequential to people conditioned and programmed by money trust monopoly media nightly news. But it is the basis for all of America's prosperity.

In 1933, FDR (Franklin Delano Roosevelt), descendent of a drug cartel with ties to Skull and Bones, Harvard and Yale endowments, violated our Constitutional Rights with Executive Order 6102 that confiscated and outlawed the gold and gold contracts that protect people and their money from government. FDR used threats of ten years in prison and a $10,000 fine (approaching a million dollars today in terms of the gold dollar) to enforce the Executive Order that bypassed Congress and was uphold by the Courts he appointed.

Once he had gotten the majority of gold other than that shipped overseas by the wealthy, he devalued the dollar 80% by revaluing it from $20 an ounce of gold to $36 an ounce of gold.

Then, as now, the claim was a cheaper dollar would jumpstart the economy.

The Dow (Dow Jones Industrials) economic indicator went from 108 in 1933 to 194 in 1937. In real terms of inflation and dollar devaluation, we did not recover to 1929 highs until 1966.

Unemployment continued to climb, then as now.

POSTMASTER: PLEASE POST IN A CONSPICUOUS PLACE.—JAMES A. FARLEY, Postmaster General

UNDER EXECUTIVE ORDER OF THE PRESIDENT

Issued April 5, 1933

all persons are required to deliver

ON OR BEFORE MAY 1, 1933

all GOLD COIN, GOLD BULLION, AND GOLD CERTIFICATES now owned by them to a Federal Reserve Bank, branch or agency, or to any member bank of the Federal Reserve System.

Executive Order

FORBIDDING THE HOARDING OF GOLD COIN, GOLD BULLION AND GOLD CERTIFICATES

[illegible]

[illegible]

This order and these regulations may be modified or revoked at any time.

FRANKLIN D ROOSEVELT

THE WHITE HOUSE,
April 5, 1933.

For Further Information Consult Your Local Bank

GOLD CERTIFICATES may be identified by the words "GOLD CERTIFICATE" appearing thereon. The serial number and the Treasury seal on the face of a GOLD CERTIFICATE are printed in YELLOW. Be careful not to confuse GOLD CERTIFICATES with other issues which are redeemable in gold but which are not GOLD CERTIFICATES. Federal Reserve Notes and United States Notes are "redeemable in gold" but are not "GOLD CERTIFICATES" and are not required to be surrendered

Special attention is directed to the exceptions allowed under Section 2 of the Executive Order

CRIMINAL PENALTIES FOR VIOLATION OF EXECUTIVE ORDER
$10,000 fine or 10 years imprisonment, or both, as provided in Section 9 of the order

W H Woodin
Secretary of the Treasury.

U.S. Government Printing Office: 1933 [illegible]

Ron Paul's 2009 to 2012 Full Audit of the Fed bills, *The Federal Reserve Transparency Act*, were passed in the House by majority votes up to 327-98 with majority public support.

His Fed Act was introduced to the Senate by his son Rand Paul as *The Federal Reserve Sunshine Act,* where it was stuck in Committee by the Senate Majority Leader for four years.

Re the economic government political corruption progress we saw fictionalized in *Die Hard with a Vengeance*, *Godfather II* and true in real life:

Personal correspondence from an International Economics Professor, TV commentator and World Affairs University Professor turned big government politician, went from ridiculing feeding frenzy at the public trough to an anti-life government funding advocate.

His family created Special Interest Tax Free Foundations opposed to those who worked to limit the size and terms of government and politics, to restore better jobs and economic growth with free markets, instead of unfair government trade agreements that benefitted mainly big business multinational monopolies.

Under his 27-years in Congress (until he died in office of cancer), after advocating term limits for others, American jobs went overseas or were replaced by mandatory taxpayer subsidized illegal immigrants, while our real standard of living was cut in half by deliberate inflation and government policy.

Media sound bite pictures and stories were so appealing and the voter turnout so low, he kept getting re-elected until his successor lightly challenged him in his last party primary, which he won.

We had been elected to public office in the 70s and had our fill of politics.

We went from Non-profits into business (highly regulated by government and politicians unless you are a campaign fund bundler).

We received enthusiastic initial response to our 1994 campaign test of the waters to Renew

Congress. Then we were subtly shunned by RINO Party elders into withdrawing for a woman candidate without political experience.

We were kept from having an accurate job description or candidate statement by a false election fraud claim by the opposition, with a *writ of mandamus* Judge friendly to the incumbent's party, who did not provide a timely transcript for decision appeal before the election.

The question remains, how can justice be impartial, when Judicial salaries are paid by government, albeit taxpayers?

Taxpayers and voters are kept well insulated from Judicial accountability, inconsistent irrational decisions, an intimidating opaque process supporting even-bigger government cloaked by soothing stealth monopoly media language talking about government investment instead of actual higher debts, spending, taxes and waste.

One successful businessman dared try to defend himself from Judicial tyranny. He was ordered into prison for contempt of court. There he was beaten up, denied proper medical care, and kept in solitary over seven years without a trial until he plea-bargained to get out of the hole. Then he was sentenced to serve five more years without credit for time served.

Ethical attorneys and judges I know became less adversarial arbitrators and mediators.

Back in the Contract with America year of 1994, the delighted incumbent sent the challenger roses with a *good luck* note. She was mauled by 2:1 D:R machine politics that included cash for union members voting dead names on voter registration lists without voter ID, according to multiple precinct witnesses.

We repeatedly asked the Governor, Attorney General, Secretary of State and Speaker of the House to legislate and implement citizen photo voter ID.

We were told by an FBI US Attorney friend that the Mexican National assassin of a Mexican Presidential candidate was illegally registered to vote in the USA. The FBI had cross-checked illegals on the INS (Immigration Naturalization Service) list versus voter registration lists.

This continues today, with government subsidized illegal votes and mandatory taxpayer funding for illegal food stamps, free education, healthcare, housing, income, prison, unemployment and the welfare state.

After the Mexican Presidential assassin was indicted and sentenced to prison, his family received taxpayer funded political asylum in a major US city.

We vowed if we ever ran as a public servant again, we would not withdraw to please party politics, suffer Congressional or Judicial harassment in silence again.

In 2012, we filed for US Senate and spent less than $1000 on the campaign as a trial run.

With only an internet campaign and a few good friends, we received more votes per dollar than other candidates.

We stood against both main party candidates who had voted for:

1) NSA (National Security Agency) Domestic Espionage without Constitutional warrants,
2) retroactive telecom immunity under the Patriot Act,
3) Drone kills on American Citizens with the NDAA (National Defense Authorization Acts),
4) Drone Civilian Casualties violating Geneva Conventions,
5) Indefinite Detention and Renditions for torture without Habeas corpus due process,
6) defacto Martial Law and Police State purchases of armored vehicles, high-powered .50 caliber weapons and SWAT teams to burn, shoot to kill "enemies of the state," fusion center operations blurring posse comitatus separation of military and police, armoured checkpoint booths
7) DHA (Department of Homeland Security) FEMA (Federal Emergency Management Agency)

detention centers with plastic coffins and purchases of 2 billion rounds of dum dum bullet hollowpoint ammo,
8) TSA felony groping with X-Rays of American citizens,
10) A Food Safety Act that was actually the Monsanto GMO (Genetically Modified Organisms) Protection Bill,
11) Retroactive immunity for vaccine companies providing mandatory inoculations without Constitutional authority,
12) Government budgets further destroying what's left of our economy and jobs

Both major party candidates of course made reassuring smooth sound-bite political statements about their hard work for environmental protection, immigration reform, jobs, the need to fight terrorism and provide national security (by invading other nations with energy resources) for "American security."

If we weren't mesmerized by the media complex, and thought about it, we realized the claims and legislative votes were nonsense a child could see through like the Emperor's Clothes.

Most Americans were simply disgusted and too busy trying to survive, to listen to, watch or think through government monopoly media propaganda.

Now, with more and more of us disabled, retired or unemployed, *We the People* are catching on with factual internet documentation (often smeared as conspiracy theory.)

For example, I actually visited a COG (Continuity of Government) shadow government office with high security entrance and government Cabinet Department doors all around the room.

My eyes were opened.

Startpage to read John Whitehead's article in Huffington Post if you think it's a conspiracy theory joke.

Where did the President go on 9-11?

Meantime, with centrally controlled government monopoly media, not many Americans know a recent president and members of his cabinet were convicted of War Crimes outside of America. He allegedly avoided international travel to Switzerland for fear of being served arrest warrants. Fewer know one Presidential family owns property in non-extraditable Paraguay near Reverend Moon's refuge ranch with aquifer and energy resources near a US military air base.

Government media ignore this or smear it as conspiracy theory even when it makes sense and is documented by numerous original sources.

As Benjamin Franklin said, "Those who sacrifice freedom for security end up with neither."

In our 2012 Nevada campaign we deliberately avoided all candidate nights, editorial panels, and public presentations with media and special interest groups. We provided only a primitive website for the Silver Senator campaign for word of mouth discussion of actual issues instead of sound-byte smears. We did not do Facebook, Tweet or any other social media.

To our great surprise, we received more votes than any other candidate who spent more to lose.

So now it's time to rock and roll, with the best opportunity for constructive electoral revolution since 1994, which eventually fizzled out when the R's out-borrowed and outspent the D's.

Two legs bad, four legs good. Four legs good, two legs better.

Recent special interest monopoly political candidates won public office with money trust monopoly media smear spin campaigns capitalizing on voter turnouts as low as the 29.7% of eligible voters who elected the President of these United States in 2012.

(58.2% of eligible voters voted, times 51.1% for the winner = 29.7%, math not reported in media.)

No wonder a recent Gallup poll found just 17% of Americans have quite a lot of confidence in the Presidency.

13% of Americans have a great deal of confidence in the Supreme Court.

Just 5% of Americans have quite a lot of confidence in Congress.

Gone are the days of political majorities and moral authorities in DC some now describe as criminal politics or gangster government.

We watched sadly as the 1% Grand Old Party Republican RINO (Republican In Name Only) left US behind, while government monopoly media smeared the Ron Paul Libertarian Blue Republican Red Democrat campaign. Paul for a time polled higher than either D or R party candidate because he appealed to the majority of Americans who do not like or trust politics as usual. Paul enjoyed more military votes than any other candidate. Servicemen like my family generations do not care to fight unjust pre-emptive wars or dishonour our Constitution.

R's were the same political party that fought slavery with Lincoln to end the Whig Slave Party.

In 2012, formerly big tent RINO R's refused to count Ron Paul Primary votes, certify Ron Paul Caucus results, or let the more popular Ron Paul seat his delegates or address our Nation at the National Convention in Tampa, Florida. It's like they wanted to lose. Perhaps the only more nonsensical thing was replacing Ron Paul's speech with Clint's talk to an empty chair.

No wonder General and President George Washington said:

"However [political parties] may now and then answer popular ends, they are likely in the course of time and things, to become potent engines, by which cunning, ambitious, and unprincipled men will be enabled to subvert the power of the people and to usurp for themselves the reins of government, destroying afterwards the very engines which have lifted them to unjust dominion."

When the 2012 General election came, it was no surprise the R candidate got 27.4% of the eligible vote, (58.2% of eligible voters voted

47.2% for him). The D candidate, as mentioned, got 29.7% of the eligible vote.

That left 53 million American citizen voters disenfranchised at home by not caring to vote for either candidate in rigged special interest elections.

Who does not want peace or prosperity? Neither big party candidate offered that.

We realized a real candidate, representing the united interests of the 99% American majority, could sweep any field of special interest candidates with enough funding to get the word out to overcome money trust monopoly media controlled by 1% special interests.

We think the old belief that Libertarians never win, they just divide or throw away the vote, is no longer true now. We are willing to prove it if we get your backing.

Many eligible voters are sick of party politics as usual. They do not even register as a party member, or register at all. Some want to avoid jury duty that may actually prevent an innocent being railroaded to jail on a plea bargain, or a special interest steam-roller over American citizens with big business criminal practices.

It is here time to state that big corporations are not people, in all states but where they are incorporated, they are foreign States our Constitution, Article I, Section 9 limits:

No Title of Nobility shall be granted by the United States: And no Person holding any Office of Profit or Trust under them, shall, without the Consent of the Congress, accept of any present, Emolument, Office, or Title, of any kind whatever, from any King, Prince, or foreign State.

By this principal, many politicians may be bribed criminals.

What could get all of US American Citizens to register and vote for a Fresh Start in politics?

A Blue Republican, Green, Independent, Libertarian Non-Partisan Red Democrat

American dream candidate can bring US, our family and friends back in thundering hordes to monitor and vote precinct polls for effective Constitutional government.

We the People want to get America and Americans back on our feet, with Constitutional limited government and public service for all.

Startpage Davy Crockett's Speech to Congress for the spirit of what we are communicating.

For national example, the 2012 Freshman incumbent in Clark County Las Vegas Nevada Congressional District 1 was previously defeated as a Freshman in District 2 after raising over $2.5 Million in 2010.

By 2013, that Freshman incumbent raised almost $6 million and won.

Much of the money was from special interests, disguised as representative government.

The two-time Freshman won the 2012 race with 66% of the vote.

What 1% controlled money trust monopoly media did not tell voters, was that only 44% of eligible voters voted in the General Election in a purportedly tight Presidential Race.

That suggests 55% of voters, a silent majority, were so turned off by politics as usual they simply did not vote for anyone, even None of the Above, let alone the minority vote winner by default.

In America, *We the People* have the numerical strength in unity to win for our majority, if we do not give up our precious vote Americans shed blood to protect for 237 years.

These 55% of eligible votes are available for the candidate who represents the majority of American citizens by limiting donations to $100 and under to avoid the 1% divide and conquer monopoly special interests that spend millions to control elections to benefit themselves.

With 257,797 active voters in Congressional District 1 (CD1), $100 an election from half the active voters raises $25,779,700 from the majority of District citizens. This overrules the $6,000,000 special interest freshman who votes for unconstitutional civil and domestic government wars on American citizens and foreign nations, claiming to prevent terrorism in Las Vegas.

Perhaps the two-time Freshman thinks *We the People* are perhaps too busy or dumb to notice there were no actual real terrorist events in Las Vegas, beyond a few trigger-happy Rambo Robo cops who belong in jail for murder.

We can prove the American majority power of Democracy in our Constitutional Republic with small donations and large numbers of united Americans.

We can win the June 2014 Primary and November 2014 General election, despite or perhaps because of the usual divide and conquer money trust monopoly media smear ads from 1% special interests that characterized recent elections.

This is true both locally and nationally. We continue with our Las Vegas example.

Clark County has a wildcard of 963,825 registered voters. This compares to 1,401,236 registered Nevada voters statewide, versus only 257,797 active voters in CD1 (Congressional District 1).

No doubt some of the 963,825 registered voters were dead or illegal aliens voted by cash paid or pressured special interest patsy shills without citizen photo voter ID.

We learned this listening to concerned citizens while walking precincts door to door. They said they could not get dead or out of state family members off the voter rolls, despite repeated requests.

Some stated they were given the day off and a list of names and precincts to vote, with cash paid for each numbered election ballot receipt.

We worked as Election Official and Precinct Judge with absentee and provisional ballots. We saw no citizen positive voter ID that would stop voter fraud. We learned how the system was rigged by special interests.

Uncounted San Francisco Absentee Ballot Boxes were found floating in the Bay. Unaudited Ohio voting machine results did not match exit polls. 100% of certain large urban Pennsylvania precincts voted for one candidate by the close.

One Libertarian friend claims 23 urban districts in America now control all elections. If so, it is only because 55% of the American voters are so mad at the usual suspect candidates they stay home. The good honest candidates are smeared by money trust monopoly media for hire. In Egypt and Iraq, with bombs going off, tanks and gunshots fired, they waited in line for days to vote until the US taxpayer funded army removed elected leaders from office.

All of these electoral corruptions invite vigorous concerned citizen activism to restore that the American right to vote is counted correctly for effective representation. That is, if *We the People* really want to take control of our country back for better days ahead for our families and future generations. *We do, don't we!*

The Rasmussen Poll found 75% of likely voters "*believe voters should be required to show photo identification, such as a driver's license, before being allowed to vote.*"

Only 12 states presently have photo voter ID.

They are vigorously opposed by the current DOJ (Department of Justice in the 1984 sense). This is rather ironic, since the DOJ and many Federal buildings require photo ID with a scan to enter.

Nevada does not yet have the photo ID voter law proposed by Democrat Secretary of State Ross Miller, which may not protect against illegal voters who have picture Driver's Licenses or government photo IDs.

While DMV (Department of Motor Vehicle) Nevada laws prohibit illegals from obtaining a picture driver's license to vote in Nevada elections, counterfeit identification documents including false social security cards, false

Resident Alien I-551 cards, false Metropolitan Police Department photo IDs and false out of state licenses with photos is big business.

Punishments for this if/when caught may be selectively enforced and prosecuted by people who benefit from higher taxes and increased government budget borrowing and spending.

If we elect Constitutional public servants for more life, liberty, peace and prosperity, governments will have no problem paying their productive employees and pensions.

Allegations were made that up to 40% of the Las Vegas vote was by illegals, throwing election results to the dogs.

A 4 November 2012 LVJR *(Las Vegas Journal Review Journal)* editorial by Glenn Cook found alleged Category E felonies involving Culinary Local 226. It stated:

"*In Nevada you never have to prove you're a citizen to register to vote or cast a ballot. Forget about showing government-issued photo identification at the polls, as several states now require."*

" You don't have to show a photo ID at any point in the process. The immigrants I met could vote Tuesday just by showing a Culinary health insurance card and a power bill. "

" One would establish identity and one would establish residence," Clark County Registrar of Voters Larry Lomax said of state standards."

" Just like every other voter in Nevada, they will not be asked to prove citizenship. "

Editorialist Cook interviewed illegals who were forced to commit perjury on their voter registrations by stating they were US citizens, who were threatened by union canvassers.

" The Culinary canvassers started seeking them out and ordering them to go vote. "

" After a few days of early voting, the union knew the immigrants still hadn't voted. So union canvassers kept visiting."

"*One of the immigrants was visited at home by a Culinary representative and said the operative made threats of deportation if no ballot was cast.*"

"*One day, when a Culinary representative was told the immigrant wasn't a citizen and wouldn't vote, things got testy. The immigrant was "in so much trouble," the Culinary operative said, according to Brenda Moraine, a local immigrant advocate who was there.*"

Front Page Magazine reported:

"*Americans for Legal Immigration Political Action Committee (ALIPAC) filed a formal complaint with the Federal Election Committee (FEC), the Nevada Secretary of State's Office, and the Clark County Board of Elections.*"

Isn't it important these government agencies do their job insuring the integrity of the elections?

"*In their complaint, ALIPAC charges that numerous illegal immigrants and non-citizens are registering and voting in federal elections that will decide which presidential candidate or political party controls the White House, [Congress] and US Senate."*

" *William Gheen, President of AlIPAC, said that the LVJR investigation is evidence that voting by illegal immigrants isn't merely a conspiracy, but a real problem."*

" *Illegal alien voters are not a conspiracy theory," said Gheen."*

"***He continued, "The information we have shows mass illegal immigrant voting in Clark County."***

Clark County includes the City of Las Vegas.

" *Gheen said that he believes that tens of thousands of illegal aliens are voting in Nevada and he even stated that at least one high-profile election was swayed by illegal immigrants."*

"*Gheen said that he believes that Harry Reid beat Sharron Angle because thousands of illegal aliens voted for Harry Reid in 2010.*"

"*He [Reid in 2010] lost every County but Clark County,*" *said Gheen of why he believes that Reid was helped by illegal aliens.*"

"*In that race, Angle filed a complaint citing voter intimidation by management at Harrah's Casino. Gheen said that a number of illegal immigrants work at that Harrah's.*"

Isn't it important that government immigration agents enforce the law against illegal employment displacing American workers and illegal voting displacing Constitutional government?

"*Gheen also said that an ALIPAC supporter from Nevada who worked as a poll worker in this cycle was dismissed from that job after complaining about illegal immigrants voting.*"

If enough Libertarian registered voters protest the status quo by donating $100 or less and turning out to vote together with monitoring polls, challenging and stopping illegal votes, we can and will prevail on behalf of 99% of Americans, leaving those dangling chads and dead illegal votes in the dust.

We are humbly talking about a peaceful electoral revolution in 2014 all over America, starting with Las Vegas.

It's time for what happens in Vegas to go National and even Global.

As a local example of what is true all over these United States:

If just one quarter of Clark County Las Vegas registered, but previously inactive voters, register Libertarian before the Tuesday 20 May 2014 cutoff on-line here:

https://nvsos.gov/sosvoterservices/Registration/step1.aspx

and hit the $100 or under Donate Button on-line here:

http://usnvrepcan.blogspot.com/

A) our American Fresh Start majority can outraise and outvote the special interests,

B) support, volunteer and vote for the Fresh Start Campaign Tuesday 10 June 2014 Libertarian Primary

C) and Tuesday 4 November 2014 General election,

D) we can raise a record $96,382,500 to get the word out to win of, for and by the American people.

We the People can change the game for the better to represent 99% of the voters with Constitutional government public service, not the usual 1% special interests now funded and represented in Congress, working against life, liberty, peace and prosperity for all Americans.

Why else were unConstitutional laws benefitting the 1% passed?

More and more Americans understand that when government says they are here to help, especially the children, they don't even know what their names, colours and needs are.

This despite monumental social media domestic espionage disguised as the Patriot Act repeatedly passed by a majority in Congress not representing their constituents or voters.

You would think more American industrialists would understand as Henry Ford did, that taking better care of your people is good business for all Americans.

In 2014, we see a Libertarian ground swell by American voters fed up with and turned off by typical divide and conquer 1% monopoly media party politics sound bites as usual.

This 10 June 2014 Primary Election and 4 November 2014 General Election, *We the People* can provide poll monitoring to prevent election fraud.

That's just two days of action in Nevada for a better America. Not bad.

Of course voter name id wins elections.

That is why we are willing to come out of Senior retirement on Social Security and Medicare to reach and register as many voters as we can by the 3 March 2014 candidate filing deadline for the June 2014 Primary, once we have enough money to get the majority message out.

Otherwise, we stay Anonymous in our PJs at home, waiting for Godot, sighing at what could have been.

So please buy and share *Fresh Start POP(2) Common Sense* with family, friends and neighbors over government cheese (LOL).

We think $100 or less and voting two days for freedom is a good investment by all for our better future.

Do you agree?

Then please share, share and share the good word of *Fresh Start 2014 POP(2) Common Sense.*

That is why we worked years with blue elephants and yellow dogs to reprise our *1994 Politics of Prosperity* into this shorter $13 (One dollar for each American colony) *Common Sense* book to recruit donations $100 and under from as many majority volunteers for a better America as possible.

We imagine our *POP Part III The Triumph* could tell gratefully after the fact how we all worked together to make the vital difference for better government, with a lot of American commitment, ingenuity, knowhow, legal pragmatic support and smart sweat, to turn America around using our Constitutional time-proven principles of Life, Liberty and the Pursuit of Happiness.

***

13 August 2013
Nevada
USA

https://nvsos.gov/sosvoterservices/Registration/step1.aspx

http://usnvrepcan.blogspot.com/

Here then, the Fresh Start Politics of Prosperity, Part II, Common Sense circa 2013

All truth passes through three stages:

"First, it is ridiculed.
Second, it is violently opposed.
Third, it is accepted as being self-evident."

Arthur Schopenhauer, German philosopher (1788 - 1860)

POLITICS OF PROSPERITY, PART II,
A COMMON SENSE FRESH START

Common Sense, By Thomas Paine

Introduction

PERHAPS the sentiments contained in the following pages, are not yet sufficiently fashionable to procure them general favor; a long habit of not thinking a thing wrong, gives it a superficial appearance of being right, and raises at first a formidable outcry in defence of custom.

But tumult soon subsides. Time makes more converts than reason.

As a long and violent abuse of power is generally the means of calling the right of it in question, (and in matters too which might never have been thought of, had not the sufferers been aggravated into the inquiry,) and as the king hath undertaken in his own right, to support our Congress in what he calls theirs, and as the good people of this country are grievously oppressed by the combination, we have an undoubted privilege to inquire into the pretensions of both, and equally to reject the usurpations of either.

In the following sheets, the author hath studiously avoided every thing which is personal among ourselves. Compliments as well as censure to individuals make no part thereof. The wise and the worthy need not the triumph of a pamphlet; and those whose sentiments are injudicious or unfriendly, will cease of themselves, unless too much pains is bestowed upon their conversion.

The cause of America is, in a great measure, the cause of all mankind.

Many circumstances have, and will arise, which are not local, but universal, and through which the principles of all lovers of mankind are affected, and in the event of which, their affections are interested.

The laying of countries desolate with fire and arms, declaring war against the natural rights of all mankind, and extirpating the defenders thereof from the face of the earth, is the concern of every man to whom nature hath given the power of feeling; of which class, regardless of party censure, is

THE AUTHOR.

Philadelphia, Feb. 14, 1776.

OF THE ORIGIN AND DESIGN OF GOVERNMENT IN GENERAL. WITH CONCISE REMARKS ON THE CONSTITUTION

SOME writers have so confounded society with government, as to leave little or no distinction between them; whereas they are not only different, but have different origins.

Society is produced by our wants, and government by our wickedness; the former promotes our happiness positively by uniting our affections, the latter negatively by restraining our vices.

The one encourages intercourse, the other creates distinctions. The first is a patron, the last a punisher.

Society in every state is a blessing, but government even in its best state is but a necessary evil in its worst state an intolerable one; for when we suffer, or are exposed to the same miseries by a government, which we might expect in a country without government, our calamities are heightened by reflecting that we furnish the means by which we suffer!

Government, like dress, is the badge of lost innocence; the palaces of kings are built on the ruins of the builders of paradise.

For were the impulses of conscience clear, uniform, and irresistibly obeyed, man would need no other lawgiver; but that not being the case, we find it necessary to surrender up a part of our property to furnish means for the protection of the rest; and this we are induced to do by the same prudence which in every other case advises us out of two evils to choose the least.

Wherefore, security being the true design and end of government, it unanswerably follows that whatever form thereof appears most likely to ensure it to us, with the least expense and greatest benefit, is preferable to all others.

In order to gain a clear and just idea of the design and end of government, let us suppose a small number of persons settled in some sequestered part of the earth, unconnected with the rest, they will then represent the first peopling of any country, or of the world.

In this state of natural liberty, society will be their first thought.

A thousand motives will excite them thereto, the strength of one man is so unequal to his wants, and his mind so unfitted for perpetual solitude, that he is soon obliged to seek assistance and relief of another, who in his turn requires the same.

Four or five united would be able to raise a tolerable dwelling in the midst of a wilderness, but one man might labor out the common period of life without accomplishing any thing; when he had felled his timber he could not remove it, nor erect it after it was removed; hunger in the mean time would urge him from his work, and every different want call him a different way.

Disease, nay even misfortune would be death, for though neither might be mortal, yet either would disable him from living, and reduce him to a state in which he might rather be said to perish than to die.

Thus necessity, like a gravitating power, would soon form our newly arrived emigrants into society, the reciprocal blessings of which, would supersede, and render the obligations of law and government unnecessary while they remained perfectly just to each other; but as nothing but heaven is impregnable to vice, it will unavoidably happen, that in proportion as they surmount the first difficulties of emigration, which bound them together in a common cause, they will begin to relax in their duty and attachment to each other; and this remissness, will point out the necessity, of establishing some form of government to supply the defect of moral virtue.

Some convenient tree will afford them a State-House, under the branches of which, the whole colony may assemble to deliberate on public matters.

It is more than probable that their first laws will have the title only of Regulations, and be enforced by no other penalty than public disesteem. In this first congress every man, by natural right will have a seat.

But as the colony increases, the public concerns will increase likewise, and the distance at which the members may be separated, will render it too inconvenient for all of them to meet on every occasion as at first, when their number was small, their habitations near, and the public concerns few and trifling.

This will point out the convenience of their consenting to leave the legislative part to be managed by a select number chosen from the whole body, who are supposed to have the same concerns at stake which those have who appointed them, and who will act in the same manner as the whole body would act were they present.

If the colony continue increasing, it will become necessary to augment the number of the representatives, and that the interest of every part of the colony may be attended to, it will be found best to divide the whole into convenient parts, each part sending its proper number; and that the elected might never form to themselves an interest separate from the electors, prudence will point out the propriety of having elections often; because as the elected might by that means return and mix again with the general body of the electors in a few months, their fidelity to the public will be secured by the prudent reflection of not making a rod for themselves.

And as this frequent interchange will establish a common interest with every part of the community, they will mutually and naturally support each other, and on this (not on the unmeaning name of king) depends the strength of government, and the happiness of the governed.

Here then is the origin and rise of government; namely, a mode rendered necessary by the inability of moral virtue to govern the world; here too is the design and end of government, viz., freedom and security.

And however our eyes may be dazzled with snow, or our ears deceived by sound; however prejudice may warp our wills, or interest darken our understanding, the simple voice of nature and of reason will say, it is right.

I draw my idea of the form of government from a principle in nature, which no art can overturn, viz., that the more simple any thing is, the less liable it is to be disordered, and the easier repaired when disordered; and with this maxim in view, I offer a few remarks on the so much boasted Congress.

That it was noble for the dark and slavish times in which it was erected is granted. When the world was overrun with tyranny the least therefrom was a glorious rescue. But that it is imperfect, subject to convulsions, and incapable of producing what it seems to promise, is easily demonstrated.

Absolute governments (through the disgrace of human nature) have this advantage with them, that they are simple; if the people suffer, they know the head from which their suffering springs, know likewise the remedy, and are not bewildered by a variety of causes and cures.

But the Congress is so exceedingly complex, that the nation may suffer for years together without being able to discover in which part the fault lies, some will say in one and some in another, and every political physician will advise a different medicine.

I know it is difficult to get over local or long standing prejudices, yet if we will suffer ourselves to examine the component parts of the Congress, we shall find them to be the base remains of two ancient tyrannies, compounded with some new democrat republican materials.

First.- The remains of monarchical tyranny in the person of the king.

Secondly.- The remains of aristocratical tyranny in the persons of the peers.

Thirdly.- The new democrat republican materials, in the persons of the commons, on whose virtue depends the freedom of America.

The two first, by being hereditary, are independent of the people; wherefore in a constitutional sense they contribute nothing towards the freedom of the state.

To say that the Constitution is a union of three powers reciprocally checking each other, is farcical, either the words have no meaning, or they are flat contradictions.

To say that the Congress is a check upon the king, presupposes two things.

First.- That the king is not to be trusted without being looked after, or in other words, that a thirst for absolute power is the natural disease of autarchy.

Secondly.- That the Congress, by being appointed for that purpose, are either wiser or more worthy of confidence than the crown.

But as the same Constitution which gives the Congress a power to check the king by withholding the supplies, gives afterwards the king a power to check the Congress, by empowering him to reject their other bills; it again supposes that the king is wiser than those whom it has already supposed to be wiser than him. A mere absurd tautology!

There is something exceedingly ridiculous in the composition of autarchy; it first excludes a man from the means of information, yet empowers him to act in cases where the highest judgment is required.

The state of a king shuts him from the world, yet the business of a king requires him to know it thoroughly; wherefore the different parts, unnaturally opposing and destroying each other, prove the whole character to be absurd and useless.

Some writers have explained the Congress thus; the king, say they, is one, the people another; the Senate are an house in behalf of the king; the Congress in behalf of the people; but this hath all the distinctions of an house divided against itself; and though the expressions be pleasantly arranged, yet when examined they appear idle and ambiguous; and it will always happen, that the nicest construction that words are capable of, when applied to the description of something which either cannot exist, or is too incomprehensible to be within the compass of description, will be words of sound only, and though they may amuse the ear, they cannot inform the mind, for this explanation includes a previous question, viz.

How came the king by a power which the people are afraid to trust, and always obliged to check? Such a power could not be the gift of a wise people, neither can any power, which needs checking, be from God; yet the provision, which the Constitution makes, supposes such a power to exist.

But the provision is unequal to the task; the means either cannot or will not accomplish the end, and the whole affair is a felo de se (felon of oneself; suicide); for as the greater weight will always carry up the less, and as all the wheels of a machine are put in motion by one, it only remains to know which power in the Constitution has the most weight, for that will govern; and though the others, or a part of them, may clog, or, as the phrase is, check the rapidity of its motion, yet so long as they cannot stop it, their endeavors will be ineffectual; the first moving power will at last have its way, and what it wants in speed is supplied by time.

That the King is this overbearing part in the Constitution needs not be mentioned, and that it derives its whole consequence merely from being the giver of places pensions is self evident, wherefore, though we have and wise enough to shut and lock a door against absolute monarchy, we at the same time have been foolish enough to put the King in possession of the key.

The prejudice of Americans, in favor of their own government by king, senate, and house, arises as much or more from national pride than reason.

Individuals are undoubtedly safer in America than in some other countries, but the will of the king is as much the law of the land in America as in th world, with this difference, that instead of proceeding directly from his mouth, it is handed to the people under the most formidable shape of an act of Congress. For the fate of Charles the First, hath only made kings more subtle not-more just.

Wherefore, laying aside all national pride and prejudice in favor of modes and forms, the plain truth is, that it is wholly owing to the Constitution of the people, and not to the Constitution of the government that the crown is not as oppressive in America as in England.

An inquiry into the constitutional errors in the American form of government is at this time highly necessary; for as we are never in a proper condition of doing justice to others, while we continue under the influence of some leading partiality, so neither are we capable of doing it to ourselves while we remain fettered by any obstinate prejudice.

And as a man, who is attached to a prostitute, is unfitted to choose or judge of a wife, so any prepossession in favor of a rotten constitution of government will disable us from discerning a good one.

OF MONARCHY AND HEREDITARY SUCCESSION

MANKIND being originally equals in the order of creation, the equality could only be destroyed by some subsequent circumstance; the distinctions of rich, and poor, may in a great measure be accounted for, and that without having recourse to the harsh, ill-sounding names of oppression and avarice.

Oppression is often the consequence, but seldom or never the means of riches; and though avarice will preserve a man from being necessitously poor, it generally makes him too timorous to be wealthy.

But there is another and greater distinction for which no truly natural or religious reason can be assigned, and that is, the distinction of men into KINGS and SUBJECTS.

Male and female are the distinctions of nature, good and bad the distinctions of heaven; but how a race of men came into the world so exalted above the rest, and distinguished like some new species, is worth enquiring into, and whether they are the means of happiness or of misery to mankind.

In the early ages of the world, according to the scripture chronology, there were no kings; the consequence of which was there were no wars; it is the pride of kings which throw mankind into confusion.

Holland without a king hath enjoyed more peace for this last century than any of the monarchial governments in Europe.

Antiquity favors the same remark; for the quiet and rural lives of the first patriarchs hath a happy something in them, which vanishes away when we come to the history of Jewish royalty.

Government by kings was first introduced into the world by the Heathens, from whom the children of Israel copied the custom.

It was the most prosperous invention the Devil ever set on foot for the promotion of idolatry.

The Heathens paid divine honors to their deceased kings, and the Christian world hath improved on the plan by doing the same to their living ones.

How impious is the title of sacred majesty applied to a worm, who in the midst of his splendor is crumbling into dust!

As the exalting one man so greatly above the rest cannot be justified on the equal rights of nature, so neither can it be defended on the authority of scripture; for the will of the Almighty, as declared by Gideon and the prophet Samuel, expressly disapproves of government by kings.

All anti-monarchial parts of scripture have been very smoothly glossed over in monarchial governments, but they undoubtedly merit the attention of countries which have their governments yet to form.

Render unto Caesar the things which are Caesar's is the scriptural doctrine of courts, yet it is no support of monarchial government, for the Jews at that time were without a king, and in a state of vassalage to the Romans.

Near three thousand years passed away from the Mosaic account of the creation, till the Jews under a national delusion requested a king.

Till then their form of government (except in extraordinary cases, where the Almighty interposed) was a kind of republic administered by a judge and the elders of the tribes.

Kings they had none, and it was held sinful to acknowledge any being under that title but the Lord of Hosts.

And when a man seriously reflects on the idolatrous homage which is paid to the persons of kings he need not wonder, that the Almighty, ever jealous of his honor, should disapprove of a form of government which so impiously invades the prerogative of heaven.

Monarchy is ranked in scripture as one of the sins of the Jews, for which a curse in reserve is denounced against them. The history of that transaction is worth attending to.

The children of Israel being oppressed by the Midianites, Gideon marched against them with a small army, and victory, through the divine interposition, decided in his favor.

The Jews elate with success, and attributing it to the generalship of Gideon, proposed making him a king, saying, Rule thou over us, thou and thy son and thy son's son.

Here was temptation in its fullest extent; not a kingdom only, but an hereditary one, but Gideon in the piety of his soul replied, I will not rule over you, neither shall my son rule over you, THE LORD SHALL RULE OVER YOU.

Words need not be more explicit; Gideon doth not decline the honor but denieth their right to give it; neither doth be compliment them with invented declarations of his thanks, but in the positive stile of a prophet charges them with disaffection to their proper sovereign, the King of Heaven.

About one hundred and thirty years after this, they fell again into the same error.

The hankering which the Jews had for the idolatrous customs of the Heathens, is something exceedingly unaccountable; but so it was, that laying hold of the misconduct of Samuel's two sons, who were entrusted with some secular concerns, they came in an abrupt and clamorous manner to Samuel, saying, Behold thou art old and thy sons walk not in thy ways, now make us a king to judge us like all the other nations.

And here we cannot but observe that their motives were bad, viz., that they might be like unto other nations, i.e., the Heathen, whereas their true glory laid in being as much unlike them as possible.

But the thing displeased Samuel when they said, give us a king to judge us; and Samuel prayed unto the Lord, and the Lord said unto Samuel, Hearken unto the voice of the people in all that they say unto thee, for they have not rejected thee, but they have rejected me, THEN I SHOULD NOT REIGN OVER THEM.

According to all the works which have done since the day; wherewith they brought them up out of Egypt, even unto this day; wherewith they have forsaken me and served other Gods; so do they also unto thee.

Now therefore hearken unto their voice, howbeit, protest solemnly unto them and show them the manner of the king that shall reign over them, i.e., not of any particular king, but the general manner of the kings of the earth, whom Israel was so eagerly copying after.

And notwithstanding the great distance of time and difference of manners, the character is still in fashion.

And Samuel told all the words of the Lord unto the people, that asked of him a king. And he said, This shall be the manner of the king that shall reign over you; he will take your sons and appoint them for himself for his chariots, and to be his horsemen, and some shall run before his chariots (this description agrees with the present mode of impressing men) and he will appoint him captains over thousands and captains over fifties, and will set them to ear his ground and to read his harvest, and to make his instruments of war, and instruments of his chariots; and he will take your daughters to be confectionaries and to be cooks and to be bakers (this describes the expense and luxury as well as the oppression of kings) and he will take your fields and your olive yards, even the best of them, and give them to his servants; and he will take the tenth of your seed, and of your vineyards, and give them to his officers and to his servants (by which we see that bribery, corruption, and favoritism are the standing vices of kings) and he will take the tenth of your men servants, and your maid servants, and your goodliest young men and your asses, and put them to his work; and he will take the tenth of your sheep, and ye shall be his servants, and ye shall cry out in that day because of your king which ye shall have chosen, AND THE LORD WILL NOT HEAR YOU IN THAT DAY.

This accounts for the continuation of monarchy; neither do the characters of the few good kings which have lived since, either sanctify the title, or blot out the sinfulness of the origin; the high encomium given of David takes no notice of him officially as a king, but only as a man after God's own heart.

Nevertheless the People refused to obey the voice of Samuel, and they said, Nay, but we will have a king over us, that we may be like all the nations, and that our king may judge us, and go out before us and fight our battles.

Samuel continued to reason with them, but to no purpose; he set before them their ingratitude, but all would not avail; and seeing them fully bent on their folly, he cried out, I will call unto the Lord, and he shall sent thunder and rain (which then was a punishment, being the time of wheat harvest) that ye may perceive and see that your wickedness is great which ye have done in the sight of the Lord, IN ASKING YOU A KING.

So Samuel called unto the Lord, and the Lord sent thunder and rain that day, and all the people greatly feared the Lord and Samuel And all the people said unto Samuel, Pray for thy servants unto the Lord thy God that we die not, for WE HAVE ADDED UNTO OUR SINS THIS EVIL, TO ASK A KING.

These portions of scripture are direct and positive. They admit of no equivocal construction. That the Almighty hath here entered his protest against monarchial government is true, or the scripture is false.

And a man hath good reason to believe that there is as much of kingcraft, as priestcraft in withholding the scripture from the public in Popish countries. For monarchy in every instance is the Popery of government.

To the evil of monarchy we have added that of hereditary succession; and as the first is a degradation and lessening of ourselves, so the second, claimed as a matter of right, is an insult and an imposition on posterity.

For all men being originally equals, no one by birth could have a right to set up his own family

in perpetual preference to all others for ever, and though himself might deserve some decent degree of honors of his contemporaries, yet his descendants might be far too unworthy to inherit them.
One of the strongest natural proofs of the folly of hereditary right in kings, is, that nature disapproves it, otherwise she would not so frequently turn it into ridicule by giving mankind an ass for a lion.

Secondly, as no man at first could possess any other public honors than were bestowed upon him, so the givers of those honors could have no power to give away the right of posterity, and though they might say, "We choose you for our head," they could not, without manifest injustice to their children, say, "that your children and your children's children shall reign over ours for ever."

Because such an unwise, unjust, unnatural compact might (perhaps) in the next succession put them under the government of a rogue or a fool.

Most wise men, in their private sentiments, have ever treated hereditary right with contempt; yet it is one of those evils, which when once established is not easily removed; many submit from fear, others from superstition, and the more powerful part shares with the king the plunder of the rest.

This is supposing the present race of kings in the world to have had an honorable origin; whereas it is more than probable, that could we take off the dark covering of antiquity, and trace them to their first rise, that we should find the first of them nothing better than the principal ruffian of some restless gang, whose savage manners of preeminence in subtlety obtained him the title of chief among plunderers; and who by increasing in power, and extending his depredations, overawed the quiet and defenseless to purchase their safety by frequent contributions.

Yet his electors could have no idea of giving hereditary right to his descendants, because such a perpetual exclusion of themselves was incompatible with the free and unrestrained principles they professed to live by.

Wherefore, hereditary succession in the early ages of monarchy could not take place as a matter of claim, but as something casual or complemental; but as few or no records were extant in those days, and traditionary history stuffed with fables, it was very easy, after the lapse of a few generations, to trump up some superstitious tale, conveniently timed, Mahomet like, to cram hereditary right down the throats of the vulgar.

Perhaps the disorders which threatened, or seemed to threaten on the decease of a leader and the choice of a new one (for elections among ruffians could not be very orderly) induced many at first to favor hereditary pretensions; by which means it happened, as it hath happened since, that what at first was submitted to as a convenience, was afterwards claimed as a right.

America, since the conquest, hath known some few good monarchs, but groaned beneath a much larger number of bad ones, yet no man in his senses can say that their claim under William the Conqueror is a very honorable one.

A bastard landing with an armed banditti, and establishing himself king of America against the consent of the natives, is in plain terms a very paltry rascally original. It certainly hath no divinity in it.

However, it is needless to spend much time in exposing the folly of hereditary right, if there are any so weak as to believe it, let them promiscuously worship the ass and lion, and welcome. I shall neither copy their humility, nor disturb their devotion.

Yet I should be glad to ask how they suppose kings came at first?

The question admits but of three answers, viz., either by lot, by election, or by usurpation.

If the first king was taken by lot, it establishes a precedent for the next, which excludes hereditary succession. Saul was by lot, yet the succession was not hereditary, neither does it appear from that transaction there was any intention it ever should.

If the first king of any country was by election, that likewise establishes a precedent for the next; for to say, that the right of all future generations is taken away, by the act of the first electors, in their choice not only of a king, but of a family of kings for ever, hath no parallel in or out of scripture but the doctrine of original sin, which supposes the free will of all men lost in Adam; and from such comparison, and it will admit of no other, hereditary succession can derive no glory.

For as in Adam all sinned, and as in the first electors all men obeyed; as in the one all mankind were subjected to Satan, and in the other to Sovereignty; as our innocence was lost in the first, and our authority in the last; and as both disable us from reassuming some former state and privilege, it unanswerably follows that original sin and hereditary succession are parallels.

Dishonorable rank! Inglorious connection! Yet the most subtle sophist cannot produce a juster simile.

As to usurpation, no man will be so hardy as to defend it; and that William the Conqueror was an usurper is a fact not to be contradicted. The plain truth is, that the antiquity of American monarchy will not bear looking into.

But it is not so much the absurdity as the evil of hereditary succession which concerns mankind.

Did it ensure a race of good and wise men it would have the seal of divine authority, but as it opens a door to the foolish, the wicked; and the improper, it hath in it the nature of oppression.

Men who look upon themselves born to reign, and others to obey, soon grow insolent; selected from the rest of mankind their minds are early poisoned by importance; and the world they act in differs so materially from the world at large, that they have but little opportunity of knowing its true interests, and when they succeed to the government are frequently the most ignorant and unfit of any throughout the dominions.

Another evil which attends hereditary succession is, that the throne is subject to be possessed by a minor at any age; all which time the regency, acting under the cover of a king, have every opportunity and inducement to betray their trust.

The same national misfortune happens, when a king worn out with age and infirmity, enters the last stage of human weakness. In both these cases the public becomes a prey to every miscreant, who can tamper successfully with the follies either of age or infancy.

The most plausible plea, which hath ever been offered in favor of hereditary succession, is, that it preserves a nation from civil wars; and were this true, it would be weighty; whereas, it is the most barefaced falsity ever imposed upon mankind.

The whole history of America disowns the fact. Kings have reigned in that distracted kingdom since the conquest, in which time there have been (including the Revolution) no less than eight civil wars and nineteen rebellions.

Wherefore instead of making for peace, it makes against it, and destroys the very foundation it seems to stand on.

The contest for monarchy and succession, between the houses of Democrat and Republican, laid America in a scene of blood for many years.

54 pitched election battles since President Adams, besides skirmishes and sieges, were fought between Democrat and Republican or their like. Twice was Democrat prisoner to Republican, who in his turn was prisoner to Democrat.

And so uncertain is the fate of war and the temper of a nation, when nothing but personal matters are the ground of a quarrel, that Democrat was taken in triumph from a prison to a palace, and Republican obliged to fly from a palace to a foreign land; yet, as sudden transitions of temper are seldom lasting, Democrat in his turn was driven from the throne, and Republican recalled to succeed him.

The Congress always followed the strongest side.

This contest began in the reign of President Adams, and was not entirely extinguished when the families were united. Including a period of 217 years.

In short, monarchy and succession politics have laid (not this or that kingdom only) but the world in blood and ashes.

'Tis a form of government which the word of God bears testimony against, and blood will attend it.

If we inquire into the business of a king, we shall find that (in some countries they have none) and after sauntering away their lives without pleasure to themselves or advantage to the nation, withdraw from the scene, and leave their successors to tread the same idle round.

In absolute monarchies the whole weight of business civil and military, lies on the king; the children of Israel in their request for a king, urged this plea "that he may judge us, and go out before us and fight our battles."

But in countries where he is neither a judge nor a general, as in America, a man would be puzzled to know what is his business.

The nearer any government approaches to a republic, the less business there is for a king.

It is somewhat difficult to find a proper name for the government of America. Some call it a democracy, some a republic; but in its present state it is unworthy of the name, because the corrupt influence of the king and his party, by having all the places in its disposal, hath so effectually swallowed up the power, and eaten out the virtue of the Congress (the republican part in the constitution) that the government of America is presently nearly as monarchical as that of the worst monarchies.

Men fall out with names without understanding them.

For it is the Democrat, Republican and not the Constitution of America which Americans and illegals glory in, viz., the liberty of choosing a house or senate from out of their own body- and it is easy to see that when the democrat or republican virtue fails, slavery ensues.

My is the constitution of America sickly, but because monarchy hath poisoned the democracy and republic, the king and his court hath engrossed the Congress?

In America a king today hath little more to do than to make war and give away places; which in plain terms, is to impoverish the nation and set it together by the ears.

A pretty business indeed for a man to be allowed $400,000 a year for salary, $3.77 Trillion for budget, and worshipped into the bargain!

Of more worth is one honest man to society, and in the sight of God, than all the crowned ruffians that ever lived.

THOUGHTS OF THE PRESENT STATE OF AMERICAN AFFAIRS

IN the following pages I offer nothing more than simple facts, plain arguments, and common sense; and have no other preliminaries to settle with the reader, than that he will divest himself of prejudice and prepossession, and suffer his reason and his feelings to determine for themselves; that he will put on, or rather that he will not put off the true character of a man, and generously enlarge his views beyond the present day.

Volumes have been written on the subject of the struggle between America and the World.

Men of all ranks have embarked in the controversy, from different motives, and with various designs; but all have been ineffectual, and the period of debate is closed.

Arms, as the last resource, decide the contest; the appeal was the choice of the king, and the World hath accepted the challenge.

It hath been reported of the late Congressman (who tho' an able minister was not without his faults) that on his being attacked in the house of Congress, on the score, that his measures were only of a temporary kind, replied, "they will last my time."

Should a thought so fatal and unmanly possess America in the present contest, the name of ancestors will be remembered by future generations with detestation.

The sun never shined on a cause of greater worth.

'Tis not the affair of a city, a country, a province, or a kingdom, but of a continent- of at least one eighth part of the habitable globe.

'Tis not the concern of a day, a year, or an age; posterity are virtually involved in the contest, and will be more or less affected, even to the end of time, by the proceedings now.

Now is the seed time of continental union, faith and honor.

The least fracture now will be like a name engraved with the point of a pin on the tender rind of a young oak; The wound will enlarge with the tree, and posterity read it in full grown characters.

By referring the matter from argument to arms, a new area for politics is struck; a new method of thinking hath arisen.

All plans, proposals, &c. prior to the nineteenth of April, i.e., to the commencement of hostilities, are like the almanacs of the last year; which, though proper then, are superseded and useless now.

Whatever was advanced by the advocates on either side of the question then, terminated in one and the same point, viz., a union; the only difference between the parties was the method of effecting it; the one proposing force, the other friendship; but it hath so far happened that the first hath failed, and the second hath withdrawn her influence.

As much hath been said of the advantages of reconciliation, which, like an agreeable dream, hath passed away and left us as we were, it is but right, that we should examine the contrary side of the argument, and inquire into some of the many material injuries which these colonies sustain, and always will sustain, by being connected with, and dependant on Great Britain.

To examine that connection and dependence, on the principles of nature and common sense, to see what we have to trust to, if separated, and what we are to expect, if dependent.

I have heard it asserted by some, that as America hath flourished under her former connection with Great Britain, that the same connection is necessary towards her future happiness, and will always have the same effect.

Nothing can be more fallacious than this kind of argument.

We may as well assert, that because a child has thrived upon milk, that it is never to have meat;

or that the first twenty years of our lives is to become a precedent for the next twenty.

But even this is admitting more than is true, for I answer roundly, that America would have flourished as much, and probably much more, had no European power had any thing to do with her.

The commerce by which she hath enriched herself are the necessaries of life, and will always have a market while eating is the custom of Europe and the World.

But she has protected us, say some.

That she hath engrossed us is true, and defended the continent at our expense as well as her own is admitted, and she would have defended Turkey from the same motive, viz., the sake of trade and dominion.

Alas! we have been long led away by ancient prejudices and made large sacrifices to superstition.
We have boasted the protection of military, without considering, that their motive was

interest not attachment; that military did not protect us from our enemies on our account, but from her enemies on her own account, from those who had no quarrel with us on any other account, and who will always be our enemies on the same account.

Let America wave her pretensions to the World, or the World throw off the dependence, and we should be at peace with the World. The miseries of war ought to warn us against the connections.

It hath lately been asserted in Congress and Court, that the states have no relation to each other but through the parent country, i.e., that Pennsylvania and the Jerseys, and so on for the rest, are colonies by the way of Washington, DC; this is certainly a very roundabout way of proving relation ship, but it is the nearest and only true way of proving enemyship, if I may so call it.

California and New York never were, nor perhaps ever will be our enemies as Americans, but as our being the subjects of Washington, DC.

But America is the parent country, say some.

Then the more shame upon her conduct.

Even brutes do not devour their young; nor savages make war upon their families; wherefore the assertion, if true, turns to her reproach; but it happens not to be true, or only partly so, and the phrase parent or mother country hath been jesuitically adopted by the king and his parasites, with a low papistical design of gaining an unfair bias on the credulous weakness of our minds.

The World is the parent country of America.

This new world hath been the asylum for the persecuted lovers off civil and religious liberty from every Part of the World.

Hither have they fled, not from the tender embraces of the mother, but from the cruelty of the monster; and it is so far true of the world, that the same tyranny which drove the first emigrants from home pursues their descendants still.

In this extensive quarter of the globe, we forget the narrow limits of our country and carry our friendship on a larger scale; we claim brotherhood with every Christian, and triumph in the generosity of the sentiment.

It is pleasant to observe by what regular gradations we surmount the force of local prejudice, as we enlarge our acquaintance with the world.

A man born in any town in America divided into precincts or parishes, will naturally associate most with his fellow parishioners (because their interests in many cases will be common) and distinguish him by the name of neighbor; if he meet him but a few miles from home, he drops the narrow idea of a street, and salutes him by the name of townsman; if he travels out of the county, and meet him in any other, he forgets the minor divisions of street and town, and calls him countryman; i.e., countyman; but if in their foreign excursions they should associate in France or any other part of the world, their local remembrance would be enlarged.

And by a just parity of reasoning, all Europeans meeting in America, or any other quarter of the globe, are countrymen; for England, Holland, Germany, or Sweden, when compared with the whole, stand in the same places on the larger scale, which the divisions of street, town, and county do on the smaller ones; distinctions too limited for continental minds.

Not one third of the inhabitants, even of this province, are of African, Asian, European, Hispanic or Middle Eastern descent.

Wherefore, I reprobate the phrase of parent or mother country applied to Africa, Asia, Europe, Latin America or the Middle East only, as being false, selfish, narrow and ungenerous.

But admitting that we were all of African, Asian, European, Hispanic or Middle Eastern descent, what does it amount to?

Nothing.

The World, being now occupied by us in the guise of fighting terrorism, extinguishes every other name and title: And to say that reconciliation is our duty, is truly farcical.

The first king of England, of the present line (William the Conqueror) was a Frenchman, and half the peers of England are descendants from the same country; wherefore by the same method of reasoning, England ought to be governed by France.

Much hath been said of the united strength of the United Nations, that in conjunction they might bid defiance to the world.

But this is mere presumption; the fate of war is uncertain, neither do the expressions mean anything; for this continent would never suffer itself to be drained of inhabitants to support the arms throughout the World.

Besides, what have we to do with setting the world at defiance?

Our plan is commerce, and that, well attended to,will secure us the peace and friendship of all; because it is the interest of all the World to have America a free port.

Our trade will always be a protection, and our gold and silver secure us from invaders.

I challenge the warmest advocate for reconciliation, to show a single advantage that this continent can reap, by being connected politically with the World.

I repeat the challenge, not a single advantage is derived.

Our corn will fetch its price in any market in the world, and our imported goods must be paid for to buy them where we will.

But the injuries and disadvantages we sustain by that connection, are without number; and our duty to mankind I at large, as well as to ourselves, instruct us to renounce the alliance: Because, any submission to, or dependence on the World, tends directly to involve this continent in World wars and quarrels; and sets us at variance with nations, who would otherwise seek our friendship, and against whom, we have neither anger nor complaint.

As the World is our market for trade, we ought to form no partial connection with any part of it.

It is the true interest of America to steer clear of Global contentions, which she never can do, while by our dependence on the World, we are made the make-weight in the scale of Global politics.

The World is too thickly planted with kingdoms to be long at peace, and whenever a war breaks out between the World and any foreign power, the trade of America goes to ruin, because of her connection with the world.

The next war may not turn out like the Past, and should it not, the advocates for reconciliation now will be wishing for separation then, because, neutrality in that case, would be a safer convoy than a man of war.

Every thing that is right or natural pleads for separation.

The blood of the slain, the weeping voice of nature cries, 'tis time to part.

Even the distance at which the Almighty hath placed the World and America, is a strong and natural proof, that the authority of the one, over the other, was never the design of Heaven.

The time likewise at which the continent was discovered, adds weight to the argument, and the manner in which it was peopled increases the force of it.

The reformation was preceded by the discovery of America, as if the Almighty graciously meant to open a sanctuary to the persecuted in future years, when their home should afford neither friendship nor safety.

The authority of the United Nations over this continent, is a form of government, which sooner or later must have an end: And a serious mind can draw no true pleasure by looking forward, under the painful and positive conviction, that what he calls "the present Congress" is merely temporary.

As parents, we can have no joy, knowing that this government is not sufficiently lasting to ensure any thing which we may bequeath to posterity: And by a plain method of argument, as we are running the next generation into debt, we ought to do the work of it, otherwise we use them meanly and pitifully.

In order to discover the line of our duty rightly, we should take our children in our hand, and fix our station a few years farther into life; that eminence will present a prospect, which a few present fears and prejudices conceal from our sight.

Though I would carefully avoid giving unnecessary offence, yet I am inclined to believe, that all those who espouse the doctrine of reconciliation, may be included within the following descriptions:

Interested men, who are not to be trusted;

weak men who cannot see;
prejudiced men who will not see;
and a certain set of moderate men,
who think better of the World than it deserves;
and this last class by an ill-judged deliberation,
will be the cause of more calamities to this
continent than all the other three.

It is the good fortune of many to live distant from the scene of sorrow; the evil is not sufficiently brought to their doors to make them feel the precariousness with which all American property is possessed.

But let our imaginations transport us for a few moments to Boston, Chicago, Detroit, Los Angeles, New York, Philadelphia or Washington DC, the seats of wretchedness will teach us wisdom, and instruct us for ever to renounce a power in whom we can have no trust.

The inhabitants of those unfortunate cities, who but a few decades ago were in ease and affluence, have now no other alternative than to stay and starve, or turn out to beg.

Endangered by the fire of their friends if they continue within the city, and plundered by the soldiery if they leave it.

In their present condition they are prisoners without the hope of redemption, and in a general attack for their relief, they would be exposed to the fury of both armies.

Men of passive tempers look somewhat lightly over the offenses of Washington DC, and, still hoping for the best, are apt to call out, Come we shall be friends again for all this.

But examine the passions and feelings of mankind.

Bring the doctrine of reconciliation to the touchstone of nature, and then tell me, whether you can hereafter love, honor, and faithfully serve the power that hath carried fire and ammo into your land?

If you cannot do all these, then are you only deceiving yourselves, and by your delay bringing ruin upon posterity.

Your future connection with DC and the world, whom you can neither love nor honor, will be forced and unnatural, and being formed only on the plan of present convenience, will in a little time fall into a relapse more wretched than the first.

But if you say, you can still pass the violations over, then I ask, Hath your house been burnt?

Hath your family or property been destroyed before your face?

Are your wife and children destitute of a bed to lie on, or bread to live on?

Have you lost a parent or a child by their hands, and yourself the ruined and wretched survivor?

If you have not, then are you not a judge of those who have.

But if you have, and can still shake hands with the murderers, then are you unworthy of the name of husband, father, friend, or lover, and whatever may be your rank or title in life, you have the heart of a coward, and the spirit of a sycophant.

This is not inflaming or exaggerating matters, but trying them by those feelings and affections which nature justifies, and without which, we should be incapable of discharging the social duties of life, or enjoying the felicities of it.

I mean not to exhibit horror for the purpose of provoking revenge, but to awaken us from fatal and unmanly slumbers, that we may pursue determinately some fixed object.

It is not in the power of Washington DC or the world to conquer America, if she do not conquer herself by delay and timidity.

The present winter is worth an age if rightly employed, but if lost or neglected, the whole continent will partake of the misfortune; and there is no punishment which that man will not deserve, be he who, or what, or where he will, that may be the means of sacrificing a season so precious and useful.

It is repugnant to reason, to the universal order of things, to all examples from the former ages, to suppose, that this continent can longer remain subject to any external power.

The most sanguine in America do not think so.

The utmost stretch of human wisdom cannot, at this time compass a plan short of separation, which can promise the continent even a year's security.

Reconciliation is and was a fallacious dream.

Nature hath deserted the connection, and Art cannot supply her place.

For, as Milton wisely expresses, "never can true reconcilement grow where wounds of deadly hate have pierced so deep."

Every quiet method for peace hath been ineffectual.

Our prayers have been rejected with disdain; and only tended to convince us, that nothing flatters vanity, or confirms obstinacy in kings more than repeated petitioning- and nothing hath contributed more than that very measure to make the kings of Europe absolute: Witness Denmark, Germany and Sweden.

Wherefore since nothing but blows will do, for God's sake, let us come to a final separation, and not leave the next generation to be cutting throats, under the violated unmeaning names of parent and child.

To say, they will never attempt it again is idle and visionary, we thought so at the repeal of the Amnesty Bailout Healthcare acts, yet a year or two undeceived us; as well me we may suppose that nations, which have been once defeated, will never renew the quarrel.

As to government matters, it is not in the powers of DC or the World to do this continent justice: The business of it will soon be too weighty, and intricate, to be managed with any tolerable degree of convenience, by a power, so distant from us, and so very ignorant of us; for if they cannot conquer us, they cannot govern us.

To be always running three or four thousand miles with a tale or a petition, waiting four or five months for an answer, which when obtained requires five or six more to explain it in, will in a few years be looked upon as folly and childishness- there was a time when it was proper, and there is a proper time for it to cease.

Small islands not capable of protecting themselves, are the proper objects for kingdoms to take under their care; but there is something very absurd, in supposing a continent to be perpetually governed by an island.

In no instance hath nature made the satellite larger than its primary planet, and as the World and America, with respect to each Other, reverse the common order of nature, it is evident they belong to different systems: DC to the World - America to itself.

I am not induced by motives of pride, party, or resentment to espouse the doctrine of separation and independence; I am clearly, positively, and conscientiously persuaded that it is the true interest of this continent to be so; that every thing short of that is mere patchwork, that it can afford no lasting felicity,- that it is leaving the sword to our children, and shrinking back at a time, when, a little more, a little farther, would have rendered this continent the glory of the earth.

As DC and the World hath not manifested the least inclination towards a compromise, we may be assured that no terms can be obtained worthy the acceptance of the continent, or any ways equal to the expense of blood and treasure we have been already put to.

The object contended for, ought always to bear some just proportion to the expense.

The removal of the North, or the whole detestable junto, is a matter unworthy the millions we have expended.

A temporary stoppage of trade, was an inconvenience, which would have sufficiently balanced the repeal of all the acts complained of, had such repeals been obtained; but if the whole continent must take up arms, if every man must be a soldier, it is scarcely worth our while to fight against a contemptible ministry only.

Dearly, dearly, do we pay for the repeal of the acts, if that is all we fight for; for in a just estimation, it is as great a folly to pay a Bunker Hill price for law, as for land.

As I have always considered the independency of this continent, as an event, which sooner or later must arrive, so from the late rapid progress of the continent to maturity, the event could not be far off.

Wherefore, on the breaking out of hostilities, it was not worth the while to have disputed a matter, which time would have finally redressed, unless we meant to be in earnest; otherwise, it is like wasting an estate of a suit at law, to regulate the trespasses of a tenant, whose lease is just expiring.

No man was a warmer wisher for reconciliation than myself, before the fatal nineteenth of April, 1775 (Massacre at Lexington), 9-11 (Massacre in Manhattan), but the moment the event of that day was made known, I rejected the hardened, sullen tempered Pharaoh for ever; and disdain the wretch, that with the pretended title of Father of his people, can unfeelingly hear of their slaughter, and composedly sleep with their blood upon his soul.

But admitting that matters were now made up, what would be the event?

I answer, the ruin of the continent. And that for several reasons:

First. The powers of governing still remaining in the hands of the king, he will have a negative over the whole legislation of this continent.

And as he hath shown himself such an inveterate enemy to liberty, and discovered such a thirst for arbitrary power, is he, or is he not, a proper man to say to these States, "You shall make no laws but what I please?"

And is there any inhabitant in America so ignorant, as not to know, that according to what is called the present Congress, that this continent can make no laws but what the king gives leave to? and is there any man so unwise, as not to see, that (considering what has happened) he will suffer no Law to be made here, but such as suit his purpose?

We may be as effectually enslaved by the want of laws in America, as by submitting to laws made for us in DC.

After matters are made up (as it is called) can there be any doubt but the whole power of the DC crown will be exerted, to keep this continent as low and humble as possible?

Instead of going forward we shall go backward, or be perpetually quarrelling or ridiculously petitioning.

We are already greater than the king wishes us to be, and will he not hereafter endeavor to make us less?

To bring the matter to one point.

Is the power who is jealous of our prosperity, a proper power to govern us?

Whoever says No to this question is an independent, for independency means no more, than, whether we shall make our own laws, or whether the king, the greatest enemy this continent hath, or can have, shall tell us, "there shall be now laws but such as I like."

But the king you will say has a negative in England; the people there can make no laws without his consent. in point of right and good order, there is something very ridiculous, that a youth of twenty-one (which hath often happened) shall say to several millions of people, older and wiser than himself, I forbid this or that act of yours to be law.

But in this place I decline this sort of reply, though I will never cease to expose the absurdity of it, and only answer, that DC being the king's residence, and America not so, make quite another case.

The king's negative here is ten times more dangerous and fatal than it can be in the World, for there he will scarcely refuse his consent to a bill for putting DC into as strong a state of defence as possible, and in America he would never suffer such a bill to be passed.

America is only a secondary object in the system of DC politics- the New World Order consults the good of this country, no farther than it answers her own purpose.

Wherefore, her own interest leads her to suppress the growth of ours in every case which doth not promote her advantage, or in the least interfere with it.

A pretty state we should soon be in under such a second-hand government, considering what has happened!

Men do not change from enemies to friends by the alteration of a name; and in order to show that reconciliation now is a dangerous doctrine, I affirm, that it would be policy in the kingdom at this time, to repeal the acts for the sake of reinstating himself in the government of the provinces; in order, that he may accomplish by craft and subtlety, in the long run, what he cannot do by force and violence in the short one.

Reconciliation and ruin are nearly related.

Secondly. That as even the best terms, which we can expect to obtain, can amount to no more than a temporary expedient, or a kind of government by guardianship, which can last no longer than till the States come of age, so the general face and state of things, in the interim, will be unsettled and unpromising.

Emigrants of property will not choose to come to a country whose form of government hangs but by a thread, and who is every day tottering on the brink of commotion and disturbance; and numbers of the present inhabitants would lay hold of the interval, to dispose of their effects, and quit America.

But the most powerful of all arguments, is, that nothing but independence, i.e., a continental form of government, can keep the peace of the continent and preserve it inviolate from civil wars.

I dread the event of a reconciliation with Britain/DC now, as it is more than probable, that it will be followed by a revolt somewhere or other, (the War of 1812, the Civil War and the Wars of Terrorism) the consequences of which may be far more fatal than all the malice of Britain/DC.

Thousands are already ruined by DC barbarity; (thousands more will probably suffer the same fate.)

Those men have other feelings than us who have nothing suffered.

All they now possess is liberty, what they before enjoyed is sacrificed to its service, and having nothing more to lose, they disdain submission.

Besides, the general temper of the States, towards a DC government, will be like that of a youth, who is nearly out of his time, they will care very little about her.

And a government which cannot preserve the peace, is no government at all, and in that case we pay our money for nothing; and pray what is it that DC can do, whose power will be wholly on paper, should a civil tumult break out the very day after reconciliation?

I have heard some men say, many of whom I believe spoke without thinking, that they dreaded independence, fearing that it would produce civil wars.

It is but seldom that our first thoughts are truly correct, and that is the case here; for there are ten times more to dread from a patched up connection than from independence.

I make the sufferers case my own, and I protest, that were I driven from house and home, my property destroyed, and my circumstances ruined, that as man, sensible of injuries, I could never relish the doctrine of reconciliation, or consider myself bound thereby.

The colonies have manifested such a spirit of good order and obedience to continental government, as is sufficient to make every reasonable person easy and happy on that head.

No man can assign the least pretence for his fears, on any other grounds, that such as are truly childish and ridiculous, viz., that one State will be striving for superiority over another.

Where there are no distinctions there can be no superiority, perfect equality affords no temptation.

The republics of Europe are all (and we may say always) in peace. Holland and Switzerland are without wars, foreign or domestic; monarchical governments, it is true, are never long at rest: the crown itself is a temptation to enterprising ruffians at home; and that degree of pride and insolence ever attendant on regal authority swells into a rupture with foreign powers, in instances where a republican government, by being formed on more natural principles, would negotiate the mistake.

If there is any true cause of fear respecting independence it is because no plan is yet laid down.

Men do not see their way out; wherefore, as an opening into that business I offer the following hints; at the same time modestly affirming, that I have no other opinion of them myself, than that they may be the means of giving rise to something better.

Could the straggling thoughts of individuals be collected, they would frequently form materials for wise and able men to improve to useful matter.

Let the assemblies be annual, with a majority elected President only. The representation more equal. Their business wholly domestic, and subject to the authority of a majority elected Congress.

Let each state be divided into six, eight, or ten, convenient districts, each district to send a proper number of delegates to congress, so that each colony send at least thirty.

The whole number in congress will be at least three hundred ninety. Each congress to sit..... and to choose a president by the following method. When the delegates are met, let a state be taken from the whole United States by lot, after which let the whole congress choose (by ballot) a President from out of the delegates of that province.

In the next Congress, let a state be taken by lot from 49 only, omitting that colony from which the president was taken in the former congress, and so proceeding on till the whole 50 shall have had their proper rotation.

And in order that nothing may pass into a law but what is satisfactorily just, not less than three fifths of the Congress to be called a majority.

He that will promote discord, under a government so equally formed as this, would join Lucifer in his revolt.

But as there is a peculiar delicacy, from whom, or in what manner, this business must first arise, and as it seems most agreeable and consistent, that it should come from some intermediate body between the governed and the governors, that is between the Congress and the people, let a Continental Conference be held, in the following manner, and for the following purpose:

A committee of 50 members of Congress, viz., one for each state.

Two members for each House of assembly, or provincial convention; and five representatives of the people at large, to be chosen in the capital city or town of each province, for, and in behalf of the whole province, by as many qualified voters as shall think proper to attend from all parts of the province for that purpose; or, if more convenient, the representatives may be chosen in two or three of the most populous parts thereof.

In this conference, thus assembled, will be united, the two grand principles of business, knowledge and power.

The members of Congress, Assemblies, or Conventions, by having had experience in national concerns, will be able and useful counsellors, and the whole, being empowered by the people will have a truly legal authority.

The conferring members being met, let their business be to frame a Constitution, Continental Charter, or Charter of the United Colonies; (answering to what is called the Magna Charta of England) fixing the number and manner of choosing members of Congress, members of Assembly, with their date of sitting, and drawing the line of business and jurisdiction between them: always remembering, that our strength is continental, not provincial:

Securing freedom and property to all men, and above all things the free exercise of religion, according to the dictates of conscience; with such other matter as is necessary for a charter to contain.

Immediately after which, the said conference to dissolve, and the bodies which shall be chosen conformable to the said charter, to be the legislators and governors of this continent for the time being: Whose peace and happiness, may God preserve, Amen.

Should any body of men be hereafter delegated for this or some similar purpose, I offer them the following extracts from that wise observer on governments Dragonetti.

"The science" says he, "of the politician consists in fixing the true point of happiness and freedom.

Those men would deserve the gratitude of ages, who should discover a mode of government that contained the greatest sum of individual happiness, with the least national expense."
- Dragonetti on Virtue and Rewards.

But where says some is the king of America? I'll tell you Friend, he reigns above, and doth not make havoc of mankind like the Royal of Britain/DC.

Yet that we may not appear to be defective even in earthly honors, let a day be solemnly set apart for proclaiming the charter; let it be brought forth placed on the divine law, the word of God; let a crown be placed thereon, by which the world may know, that so far as we approve of monarchy, that in America the law is king.

For as in absolute governments the king is law, so in free countries the law ought to be king; and there ought to be no other.

But lest any ill use should afterwards arise, let the crown at the conclusion of the ceremony be demolished, and scattered among the people whose right it is.

A government of our own is our natural right: And when a man seriously reflects on the precariousness of human affairs, he will become convinced, that it is in finitely wiser and safer, to form a Constitution of our own in a cool deliberate manner, while we have it in our power, than to trust such an interesting event to time and chance.

If we omit it now, some Massenello* (A fisherman of Naples who aroused his countrymen against Spanish oppression, stirred them to revolt, and became king- all in one day.) may hereafter arise, who laying hold of popular disquietudes, may collect together the desperate and the discontented, and by assuming to themselves the powers of government, may sweep away the liberties of the continent like a deluge.

Should the government of America return again into the hands of a king, the tottering situation of things, will be a temptation for some desperate adventurer to try his fortune; and in such a case, what relief can kings give?

Ere she could hear the news the fatal business might be done, and ourselves suffering like the wretched Britons under the oppression of the Conqueror. Ye that oppose independence now, ye know not what ye do; ye are opening a door to eternal tyranny, by keeping vacant the seat of government.

(*Thomas Anello, otherwise Massenello, a fisherman of Naples, who after spiriting up his countrymen in the public market place, against the oppression of the Spaniards, to whom the place was then subject, prompted them to revolt, and in the space of a day became king.)

There are thousands and tens of thousands; who would think it glorious to expel from the continent, that barbarous and hellish power, which hath stirred up the Indians and Negroes to destroy us; the cruelty hath a double guilt, it is dealing brutally by us, and treacherously by them.

To talk of friendship with those in whom our reason forbids us to have faith, and our affections, (wounded through a thousand pores) instruct us to detest, is madness and folly.

Every day wears out the little remains of kindred between us and them, and can there be any reason to hope, that as the relationship expires, the affection will increase, or that we shall agree better, when we have ten times more and greater concerns to quarrel over than ever?

Ye that tell us of harmony and reconciliation, can ye restore to us the time that is past?

Can ye give to prostitution its former innocence?

Neither can ye reconcile the New World Order and America.

The last cord now is broken, the people of the New World Order are presenting addresses against us.

There are injuries which nature cannot forgive; she would cease to be nature if she did.

As well can the lover forgive the ravisher of his mistress, as the continent forgive the murders of the NWO.

The Almighty hath implanted in us these inextinguishable feelings for good and wise purposes.

They are the guardians of his image in our hearts. They distinguish us from the herd of common animals.

The social compact would dissolve, and justice be extirpated the earth, or have only a casual existence were we callous to the touches of affection.

The robber and the murderer, would often escape unpunished, did not the injuries which our tempers sustain, provoke us into justice.

O ye that love mankind!

Ye that dare oppose, not only the tyranny, but the tyrant, stand forth!

Every spot of the old world is overrun with oppression.

Freedom hath been hunted round the globe.

Asia, and Africa have long expelled her. Europe regards her like a stranger, and the New World Order hath given her warning to depart.

O! receive the fugitive, and prepare in time an asylum for mankind.

OF THE PRESENT ABILITY OF AMERICA, WITH SOME MISCELLANEOUS REFLECTIONS

I HAVE never met with a man, either in England or America, who hath not confessed his opinion, that a separation between the countries, would take place one time or other.

And there is no instance in which we have shown less judgment, than in endeavoring to describe, what we call, the ripeness or fitness of the Continent for independence.

As all men allow the measure, and vary only in their opinion of the time, let us, in order to remove mistakes, take a general survey of things and endeavor if possible, to find out the very time. But we need not go far, the inquiry ceases at once, for the time hath found us. The general concurrence, the glorious union of all things prove the fact.

It is not in numbers but in unity, that our great strength lies; yet our present numbers are sufficient to repel the force of all the world.

The Continent hath, at this time, the largest body of armed and disciplined men of any power under Heaven; and is just arrived at that pitch of strength, in which no single colony is able to support itself, and the whole, who united can accomplish the matter, and either more, or, less than this, might be fatal in its effects.

Our land force is already sufficient, and as to naval affairs, we cannot be insensible, that the NWO would never suffer an American man of war to be built while the continent remained in her hands.

Wherefore we should be no forwarder an hundred years hence in that branch, than we are now; but the truth is, we should be less so, because the timber of the country is every day diminishing, and that which will remain at last, will be far off and difficult to procure.

Were the continent crowded with inhabitants, her sufferings under the present circumstances would be intolerable.

The more sea port towns we had, the more should we have both to defend and to lose.

Our present numbers are so happily proportioned to our wants, that no man need be idle.

The diminution of trade affords an army, and the necessities of an army create a new trade.

Debts we have none; and whatever we may contract on this account will serve as a glorious memento of our virtue.

Can we but leave posterity with a settled form of government, an independent constitution of its own, the purchase at any price will be cheap.

But to expend millions, billions and trillions for the sake of getting a few acts repealed, and routing the present ministry only, is unworthy the charge, and is using posterity with the utmost cruelty; because it is leaving them the great work to do, and a debt upon their backs, from which they derive no advantage. Such a thought is unworthy a man of honor, and is the true characteristic of a narrow heart and a peddling politician.

The debt we may contract doth not deserve our regard if the work be but accomplished.

No nation ought to be without a debt. A national debt is a national bond; and when it bears no interest, is in no case a grievance.

Britain is oppressed with a debt of upwards of one hundred and forty millions sterling, for which she pays upwards of four millions interest. And as a compensation for her debt, she has a large navy; America is without a debt, and without a navy; yet for the twentieth part of the English national debt, could have a navy as large again. The navy of England is not worth, at this time, more than three millions and a half sterling.

The first and second editions of this pamphlet were published without the following calculations, which are now given as a proof that the above estimation of the navy is a just one. (See Entick's naval history, intro. page 56.)

The charge of building a ship of each rate, and furnishing her with masts, yards, sails and rigging, together with a proportion of eight months boatswain's and carpenter's sea-stores, as calculated by Mr. Burchett, Secretary to the navy, is as follows:

For a ship of 100 guns	£35,553
90	£29,886
80	£23,638
70	£17,785
60	£14,197
50	£10,606
40	£7,558
30	£5,846
20	£3,710

And from hence it is easy to sum up the value, or cost rather, of the whole British navy, which in the year 1757, when it was as its greatest glory consisted of the following ships and guns:

Ships	Guns	Cost of one	Cost of all
6	100	£35,533	£213,318
12	90	£29,886	£358,632
12	80	£23,638	£283,656
43	70	£17,785	£746,755
35	60	£14,197	£496,895
40	50	£10,606	£424,240
45	40	£7,758	£344,110
58	20	£3,710	£215,180

85 Sloops, bombs,
and fireships, one another £2,000
£170,000

Cost £3,266,786
Remains for guns £229,214
Total £3,500,000

No country on the globe is so happily situated, so internally capable of raising a fleet as America. Tar, timber, iron, and cordage are her natural produce. We need go abroad for nothing. Whereas the Dutch, who make large profits by hiring out their ships of war to the Spaniards and Portuguese, are obliged to import most of the materials they use.

We ought to view the building a fleet as an article of commerce, it being the natural manufactory of this country. It is the best money we can lay out. A navy when finished is worth more than it cost. And is that nice point in national policy, in which commerce and protection are united. Let us build; if we want them not, we can sell; and by that means replace our paper currency with ready gold and silver.

In point of manning a fleet, people in general run into great errors; it is not necessary that one-fourth part should be sailors. The privateer Terrible, Captain Death, stood the hottest engagement of any ship last war, yet had not twenty sailors on board, though her complement of men was upwards of two hundred.

A few able and social sailors will soon instruct a sufficient number of active landsmen in the common work of a ship. Wherefore, we never can be more capable to begin on maritime matters than now, while our timber is standing, our fisheries blocked up, and our sailors and shipwrights out of employ.

Men of war of seventy and eighty guns were built forty years ago in New England, and why not the same now? Ship building is America's greatest pride, and in which, she will in time excel the whole world.

The great empires of the east are mostly inland, and consequently excluded from the possibility of rivalling her. Africa is in a state of barbarism; and no power in Europe, hath either such an extent or coast, or such an internal supply of materials. Where nature hath given the one, she has withheld the other; to America only hath she been liberal of both. The vast empire of Russia is almost shut out from the sea; wherefore, her boundless forests, her tar, iron, and cordage are only articles of commerce.

In point of safety, ought we to be without a fleet? We are not the little people now, which we were sixty years ago; at that time we might have trusted our property in the streets, or fields rather; and slept securely without locks or bolts to our doors or windows.

The case now is altered, and our methods of defence ought to improve with our increase of property. A common pirate, twelve months ago, might have come up the Delaware, and laid the city of Philadelphia under instant contribution, for what sum he pleased; and the same might have happened to other places.

Nay, any daring fellow, in a brig of fourteen or sixteen guns, might have robbed the whole Continent, and carried off half a million of gold. These are circumstances which demand our attention, and point out the necessity of naval protection.

Some, perhaps, will say, that after we have made it up with Britain, she will protect us.

Can we be so unwise as to mean, that she shall keep a navy in our harbors for that purpose? Common sense will tell us, that the power which hath endeavored to subdue us, is of all others the most improper to defend us.

Conquest may be effected under the pretence of friendship; and ourselves, after a long and brave resistance, be at last cheated into slavery. And if her ships are not to be admitted into our harbors, I would ask, how is she to protect us? A navy three or four thousand miles off can be of little use, and on sudden emergencies, none at all.

Wherefore, if we must hereafter protect ourselves, why not do it for ourselves? Why do it for another?

The English list of ships of war is long and formidable, but not a tenth part of them are at any one time fit for service, numbers of them not in being; yet their names are pompously continued in the list, if only a plank be left of the ship: and not a fifth part, of such as are fit for service, can be spared on any one station at one time.

The East, and West Indies, Mediterranean, Africa, and other parts over which Britain extends her claim, make large demands upon her navy. From a mixture of prejudice and inattention, we have contracted a false notion respecting the navy of England, and have talked as if we should have the whole of it to encounter at once, and for that reason, supposed that we must have one as large; which not being instantly practicable, have been made use of by a set of disguised tories to discourage our beginning thereon.

Nothing can be farther from truth than this; for if America had only a twentieth part of the naval force of Britain, she would be by far an over match for her; because, as we neither have, nor claim any foreign dominion, our whole force would be employed on our own coast, where we should, in the long run, have two to one the advantage of those who had three or four thousand miles to sail over, before they could attack us, and the same distance to return in order to refit and recruit.

And although Britain by her fleet, hath a check over our trade to Europe, we have as large a one over her trade to the West Indies, which, by laying in the neighborhood of the Continent, is entirely at its mercy.

Some method might be fallen on to keep up a naval force in time of peace, if we should not judge it necessary to support a constant navy.

If premiums were to be given to merchants, to build and employ in their service, ships mounted with twenty, thirty, forty, or fifty guns, (the premiums to be in proportion to the loss of bulk to the merchants) fifty or sixty of those ships, with a few guard ships on constant duty, would keep up a sufficient navy, and that without burdening ourselves with the evil so loudly complained of in England, of suffering their fleet, in time of peace to lie rotting in the docks.

To unite the sinews of commerce and defence is sound policy; for when our strength and our riches, play into each other's hand, we need fear no external enemy.

In almost every article of defence we abound.

Hemp flourishes even to rankness, so that we need not want cordage. Our iron is superior to that of other countries. Our small arms equal to any in the world.

Cannon we can cast at pleasure. Saltpetre and gunpowder we are every day producing.

Our knowledge is hourly improving.

Resolution is our inherent character, and courage hath never yet forsaken us.

Wherefore, what is it that we want? Why is it that we hesitate?

From Britain we can expect nothing but ruin. If she is once admitted to the government of America again, this Continent will not be worth living in. Jealousies will be always arising; insurrections will be constantly happening; and who will go forth to quell them? Who will venture his life to reduce his own countrymen to a foreign obedience?

The difference between Pennsylvania and Connecticut, respecting some unlocated lands, shows the insignificance of a British government, and fully proves, that nothing but Continental authority can regulate Continental matters.

Another reason why the present time is preferable to all others, is, that the fewer our numbers are, the more land there is yet unoccupied, which instead of being lavished by the king on his worthless dependents, may be hereafter applied, not only to the discharge of the present debt, but to the constant support of government. No nation under heaven hath such an advantage as this.

The infant state of the Colonies, as it is called, so far from being against, is an argument in favor of independence.

We are sufficiently numerous, and were we more so, we might be less united.

It is a matter worthy of observation, that the more a country is peopled, the smaller their armies are. In military numbers, the ancients far exceeded the moderns: and the reason is evident, for trade being the consequence of population, men become too much absorbed thereby to attend to anything else.

Commerce diminishes the spirit, both of patriotism and military defence.

And history sufficiently informs us, that the bravest achievements were always accomplished in the non-age of a nation. With the increase of commerce England hath lost its spirit. The city of London, notwithstanding its numbers, submits to continued insults with the patience of a coward.
The more men have to lose, the less willing are they to venture. The rich are in general slaves to fear, and submit to courtly power with the trembling duplicity of a spaniel.

Youth is the seed-time of good habits, as well in nations as in individuals.

It might be difficult, if not impossible, to form the Continent into one government half a century hence.

The vast variety of interests, occasioned by an increase of trade and population, would create confusion.

Colony would be against colony. Each being able might scorn each other's assistance: and while the proud and foolish gloried in their little distinctions, the wise would lament that the union had not been formed before.

Wherefore, the present time is the true time for establishing it. The intimacy which is contracted in infancy, and the friendship which is formed in misfortune, are, of all others, the most lasting and unalterable. Our present union is marked with both these characters: we are young, and we have been distressed; but our concord hath withstood our troubles, and fixes a memorable area for posterity to glory in.

The present time, likewise, is that peculiar time, which never happens to a nation but once, viz., the time of forming itself into a government.

Most nations have let slip the opportunity, and by that means have been compelled to receive laws from their conquerors, instead of making laws for themselves.

First, they had a king, and then a form of government; whereas, the articles or charter of government, should be formed first, and men delegated to execute them afterwards: but from the errors of other nations, let us learn wisdom, and lay hold of the present opportunity- to begin government at the right end.

When William the Conqueror subdued England he gave them law at the point of the sword; and until we consent that the seat of government in America, be legally and authoritatively occupied, we shall be in danger of having it filled by some fortunate ruffian, who may treat us in the same manner, and then, where will be our freedom? where our property?

As to religion, I hold it to be the indispensable duty of all government, to protect all conscientious professors thereof, and I know of no other business which government hath to do therewith.

Let a man throw aside that narrowness of soul, that selfishness of principle, which the niggards of all professions are so unwilling to part with, and he will be at once delivered of his fears on that head.

Suspicion is the companion of mean souls, and the bane of all good society.

For myself I fully and conscientiously believe, that it is the will of the Almighty, that there should be diversity of religious opinions among us: It affords a larger field for our Christian kindness.

Were we all of one way of thinking, our religious dispositions would want matter for probation; and on this liberal principle, I look on the various denominations among us, to be like children of the same family, differing only, in what is called their Christian names.

Earlier in this work, I threw out a few thoughts on the propriety of a Continental Charter, (for I only presume to offer hints, not plans) and in this place, I take the liberty of rementioning the subject, by observing, that a charter is to be understood as a bond of solemn obligation, which the whole enters into, to support the right of every separate part, whether of religion, personal freedom, or property. A firm bargain and a right reckoning make long friends.

In a former page I likewise mentioned the necessity of a large and equal representation; and there is no political matter which more deserves our attention. A small number of electors, or a small number of representatives, are equally dangerous. But if the number of the representatives be not only small, but unequal, the danger is increased.

As an instance of this, I mention the following; when the Associators petition was before the House of Assembly of Pennsylvania; twenty-eight members only were present, all the Bucks County members, being eight, voted against it, and had seven of the Chester members done the same, this whole province had been governed by two counties only, and this danger it is always exposed to. The unwarrantable stretch likewise, which that house made in their last sitting, to gain an undue authority over the delegates of that province, ought to warn the people at large, how they trust power out of their own hands. A set of instructions for the Delegates were put together, which in point of sense and business would have dishonored a school-boy, and after being approved by a few, a very few without doors, were carried into the house, and there passed in behalf of the whole colony; whereas, did the whole colony know, with what ill-will that House hath entered on some necessary public measures, they would not hesitate a moment to think them unworthy of such a trust.

Immediate necessity makes many things convenient, which if continued would grow into oppressions.

Expedience and right are different things. When the calamities of America required a consultation, there was no method so ready, or at that time so proper, as to appoint persons from the several Houses of Assembly for that purpose and the wisdom with which they have proceeded hath preserved this continent from ruin.

But as it is more than probable that we shall never be without a Congress, every well-wisher to good order, must own, that the mode for choosing members of that body, deserves consideration. And I put it as a question to those, who make a study of mankind, whether representation and election is not too great a power for one and the same body of men to possess? When we are planning for posterity, we ought to remember that virtue is not hereditary.

It is from our enemies that we often gain excellent maxims, and are frequently surprised into reason by their mistakes.

Mr. Cornwall (one of the Lords of the Treasury) treated the petition of the New York Assembly with contempt, because that House, he said, consisted but of twenty-six members, which trifling number, he argued, could not with decency be put for the whole. We thank him for his involuntary honesty.*

*Those who would fully understand of what great consequence a large and equal representation is to a state, should read Burgh's political Disquisitions.

To conclude: However strange it may appear to some, or however unwilling they may be to think so, matters not, but many strong and striking reasons may be given, to show, that nothing can settle our affairs so expeditiously as an open and determined declaration for independence. Some of which are:

First. It is the custom of nations, when any two are at war, for some other powers, not engaged in the quarrel, to step in as mediators, and bring about the preliminaries of a peace: but while America calls herself the subject of Great Britain, no power, however well disposed she may be, can offer her mediation. Wherefore, in our present state we may quarrel on for ever.

Secondly. It is unreasonable to suppose, that France or Spain will give us any kind of assistance, if we mean only to make use of that assistance for the purpose of repairing the breach, and strengthening the connection between Britain and America; because, those powers would be sufferers by the consequences.

Thirdly. While we profess ourselves the subjects of Britain, we must, in the eye of foreign nations, be considered as rebels. The precedent is somewhat dangerous to their peace, for men to be in arms under the name of subjects; we on the spot, can solve the paradox: but to unite resistance and subjection, requires an idea much too refined for common understanding.

Fourthly. Were a manifesto to be published, and despatched to foreign courts, setting forth the miseries we have endured, and the peaceable methods we have ineffectually used for redress; declaring, at the same time, that not being able, any longer to live happily or safely under the cruel disposition of the British court, we had been driven to the necessity of breaking off all connection with her; at the same time assuring all such courts of our peaceable disposition towards them, and of our desire of entering into trade with them. Such a memorial would produce more good effects to this Continent, than if a ship were freighted with petitions to Britain.

Under our present denomination of British subjects we can neither be received nor heard abroad: The custom of all courts is against us, and will be so, until, by an independence, we take rank with other nations.

These proceedings may at first appear strange and difficult; but, like all other steps which we have already passed over, will in a little time become familiar and agreeable; and, until an independence is declared, the continent will feel itself like a man who continues putting off some unpleasant business from day to day, yet knows it must be done, hates to set about it, wishes it over, and is continually haunted with the thoughts of its necessity.

APPENDIX

SINCE the publication of the first edition of this pamphlet, or rather, on the same day on which it came out, the king's speech made its appearance in this city. Had the spirit of prophecy directed the birth of this production, it could not have brought it forth, at a more seasonable juncture, or a more necessary time. The bloody-mindedness of the one, show the necessity of pursuing the doctrine of the other. Men read by way of revenge. And the speech instead of terrifying, prepared a way for the manly principles of independence.

Ceremony, and even, silence, from whatever motive they may arise, have a hurtful tendency, when they give the least degree of countenance to base and wicked performances; wherefore, if this maxim be admitted, it naturally follows, that the king's speech, as being a piece of finished villainy, deserved, and still deserves, a general execration both by the congress and the people.

Yet as the domestic tranquility of a nation, depends greatly on the chastity of what may properly be called national manners, it is often better, to pass some things over in silent disdain, than to make use of such new methods of dislike, as might introduce the least innovation, on that guardian of our peace and safety.

And perhaps, it is chiefly owing to this prudent delicacy, that the king's speech, hath not before now, suffered a public execution. The speech if it may be called one, is nothing better than a wilful audacious libel against the truth, the common good, and the existence of mankind; and is a formal and pompous method of offering up human sacrifices to the pride of tyrants.

But this general massacre of mankind, is one of the privileges, and the certain consequences of kings; for as nature knows them not, they know not her, and although they are beings of our own creating, they know not us, and are become the gods of their creators. The speech hath one good quality, which is, that it is not calculated to deceive, neither can we, even if we would, be deceived by it.

Brutality and tyranny appear on the face of it. It leaves us at no loss: And every line convinces, even in the moment of reading, that He, who hunts the woods for prey, the naked and untutored Indian, is less a savage than the king of Britain.

Sir John Dalrymple, the putative father of a whining jesuitical piece, fallaciously called, The address of the people of ENGLAND to the inhabitants of America, hath, perhaps from a vain supposition, that the people here were to be frightened at the pomp and description of a king, given, (though very unwisely on his part) the real character of the present one: "But," says this writer, "if you are inclined to pay compliments to an administration, which we do not complain of," (meaning the Marquis of Rockingham's at the repeal of the Stamp Act) "it is very unfair in you to withhold them from that prince, by whose NOD ALONE they were permitted to do anything."

This is toryism with a witness! Here is idolatry even without a mask: And he who can calmly hear, and digest such doctrine, hath forfeited his claim to rationality an apostate from the order of manhood; and ought to be considered- as one, who hath, not only given up the proper dignity of a man, but sunk himself beneath the rank of animals, and contemptibly crawl through the world like a worm.

However, it matters very little now, what the king of England either says or does; he hath wickedly broken through every moral and human obligation, trampled nature and conscience beneath his feet; and by a steady and constitutional spirit of insolence and cruelty, procured for himself an universal hatred.

It is now the interest of America to provide for herself. She hath already a large and young family, whom it is more her duty to take care of, than to be granting away her property, to support a power who is become a reproach to the names of men and Christians.

Ye, whose office it is to watch over the morals of a nation, of whatsoever sect or denomination ye are of, as well as ye, who are more immediately the guardians of the public liberty, if ye wish to preserve your native country uncontaminated by European corruption, ye must in secret wish a separation.

But leaving the moral part to private reflection, I shall chiefly confine my farther remarks to the following heads:

First. That it is the interest of America to be separated from Britain.

Secondly. Which is the easiest and most practicable plan, reconciliation or independence? with some occasional remarks.

In support of the first, I could, if I judged it proper, produce the opinion of some of the ablest and most experienced men on this continent; and whose sentiments, on that head, are not yet publicly known. It is in reality a self-evident position: For no nation in a state of foreign dependence, limited in its commerce, and cramped and fettered in its legislative powers, can ever arrive at any material eminence.

America doth not yet know what opulence is; and although the progress which she hath made stands unparalleled in the history of other nations, it is but childhood, compared with what she would be capable of arriving at, had she, as she ought to have, the legislative powers in her own hands.

England is, at this time, proudly coveting what would do her no good, were she to accomplish it; and the Continent hesitating on a matter, which will be her final ruin if neglected.

It is the commerce and not the conquest of America, by which England is to be benefited, and that would in a great measure continue, were the countries as independent of each other as France and Spain; because in many articles, neither can go to a better market.

But it is the independence of this country on Britain or any other which is now the main and only object worthy of contention, and which, like all other truths discovered by necessity, will appear clearer and stronger every day.

First. Because it will come to that one time or other. Secondly. Because the longer it is delayed the harder it will be to accomplish.

I have frequently amused myself both in public and private companies, with silently remarking the spacious errors of those who speak without reflecting. And among the many which I have heard, the following seems the most general, viz., that had this rupture happened forty or fifty years hence, instead of now, the Continent would have been more able to have shaken off the dependence.

To which I reply, that our military ability at this time, arises from the experience gained in the last war, and which in forty or fifty years time, would have been totally extinct. The Continent, would not, by that time, have had a General, or even a military officer left; and we, or those who may succeed us, would have been as ignorant of martial matters as the ancient Indians: And this single position, closely attended to, will unanswerably prove, that the present time is preferable to all others: The argument turns thus- at the conclusion of the last war, we had experience, but wanted numbers; and forty or fifty years hence, we should have numbers, without experience; wherefore, the proper point of time, must be some particular point between the two extremes, in which a sufficiency of the former remains, and a proper increase of the latter is obtained: And that point of time is the present time.

The reader will pardon this digression, as it does not properly come under the head I first set out with, and to which I again return by the following position, viz.:

Should affairs be patched up with Britain, and she to remain the governing and sovereign power of America, (which as matters are now circumstanced, is giving up the point entirely) we shall deprive ourselves of the very means of sinking the debt we have or may contract.

The value of the back lands which some of the provinces are clandestinely deprived of, by the unjust extension of the limits of Canada, valued only at five pounds sterling per hundred acres, amount to upwards of twenty-five millions, Pennsylvania currency; and the quit-rents at one penny sterling per acre, to two millions yearly.

It is by the sale of those lands that the debt may be sunk, without burden to any, and the quit-rent reserved thereon, will always lessen, and in time, will wholly support the yearly expense of government. It matters not how long the debt is in paying, so that the lands when sold be applied to the discharge of it, and for the execution of which, the Congress for the time being, will be the continental trustees.

I proceed now to the second head, viz. Which is the earliest and most practicable plan, reconciliation or independence? with some occasional remarks.

He who takes nature for his guide is not easily beaten out of his argument, and on that ground, I answer generally- That INDEPENDENCE being a SINGLE SIMPLE LINE, contained within ourselves; and reconciliation, a matter exceedingly perplexed and complicated, and in which, a treacherous capricious court is to interfere, gives the answer without a doubt.

The present state of America is truly alarming to every man who is capable of reflection. Without law, without government, without any other mode of power than what is founded on, and granted by courtesy. Held together by an unexampled concurrence of sentiment, which is nevertheless subject to change, and which every secret enemy is endeavoring to dissolve.

Our present condition, is, legislation without law; wisdom without a plan; a constitution without a name; and, what is strangely astonishing, perfect Independence contending for dependence.

The instance is without a precedent; the case never existed before; and who can tell what may be the event? The property of no man is secure in the present unbraced system of things.

The mind of the multitude is left at random, and feeling no fixed object before them, they pursue such as fancy or opinion starts. Nothing is criminal; there is no such thing as treason; wherefore, every one thinks himself at liberty to act as he pleases. The tories dared not to have assembled offensively, had they known that their lives, by that act were forfeited to the laws of the state. A line of distinction should be drawn, between English soldiers taken in battle, and inhabitants of America taken in arms. The first are prisoners, but the latter traitors. The one forfeits his liberty the other his head.

Notwithstanding our wisdom, there is a visible feebleness in some of our proceedings which gives encouragement to dissensions. The Continental Belt is too loosely buckled. And if something is not done in time, it will be too late to do any thing, and we shall fall into a state, in which, neither reconciliation nor independence will be practicable.

The king and his worthless adherents are got at their old game of dividing the continent, and there are not wanting among us printers, who will be busy spreading specious falsehoods.

The artful and hypocritical letter which appeared a few months ago in two of the New York papers, and likewise in two others, is an evidence that there are men who want either judgment or honesty.

It is easy getting into holes and corners and talking of reconciliation: But do such men seriously consider, how difficult the task is, and how dangerous it may prove, should the Continent divide thereon.

Do they take within their view, all the various orders of men whose situation and circumstances, as well as their own, are to be considered therein. Do they put themselves in the place of the sufferer whose all is already gone, and of the soldier, who hath quitted all for the defence of his country. If their ill judged moderation be suited to their own private situations only, regardless of others, the event will convince them, that "they are reckoning without their Host."

Put us, says some, on the footing we were in the year 1763: To which I answer, the request is not now in the power of Britain to comply with, neither will she propose it; but if it were, and even should be granted, I ask, as a reasonable question, By what means is such a corrupt and faithless court to be kept to its engagements?

Another parliament, nay, even the present, may hereafter repeal the obligation, on the pretence of its being violently obtained, or unwisely granted; and in that case, Where is our redress? No going to law with nations; cannon are the barristers of crowns; and the sword, not of justice, but of war, decides the suit.

To be on the footing of 1763, it is not sufficient, that the laws only be put on the same state, but, that our circumstances, likewise, be put on the same state; our burnt and destroyed towns repaired or built up, our private losses made good, our public debts (contracted for defence) discharged; otherwise, we shall be millions worse than we were at that enviable period. Such a request had it been complied with a year ago, would have won the heart and soul of the continent- but now it is too late, "the Rubicon is passed."

Besides the taking up arms, merely to enforce the repeal of a pecuniary law, seems as unwarrantable by the divine law, and as repugnant to human feelings, as the taking up arms to enforce obedience thereto.

The object, on either side, doth not justify the ways and means; for the lives of men are too valuable to be cast away on such trifles. It is the violence which is done and threatened to our persons; the destruction of our property by an armed force; the invasion of our country by fire and sword, which conscientiously qualifies the use of arms: And the instant, in which such a mode of defence became necessary, all subjection to Britain ought to have ceased; and the independency of America should have been considered, as dating its area from, and published by, the first musket that was fired against her.

This line is a line of consistency; neither drawn by caprice, nor extended by ambition; but produced by a chain of events, of which the colonies were not the authors.

I shall conclude these remarks, with the following timely and well intended hints, We ought to reflect, that there are three different ways by which an independency may hereafter be effected; and that one of those three, will one day or other, be the fate of America, viz.

By the legal voice of the people in congress; by a military power; or by a mob: It may not always happen that our soldiers are citizens, and the multitude a body of reasonable men; virtue, as I have already remarked, is not hereditary, neither is it perpetual.

Should an independency be brought about by the first of those means, we have every opportunity and every encouragement before us, to form the noblest, purest constitution on the face of the earth. We have it in our power to begin the world over again.

A situation, similar to the present, hath not happened since the days of Noah until now. The birthday of a new world is at hand, and a race of men perhaps as numerous as all Europe contains, are to receive their portion of freedom from the event of a few months.

The reflection is awful- and in this point of view, how trifling, how ridiculous, do the little, paltry cavillings, of a few weak or interested men appear, when weighed against the business of a world.

Should we neglect the present favorable and inviting period, and an independence be hereafter effected by any other means, we must charge the consequence to ourselves, or to those rather, whose narrow and prejudiced souls, are habitually opposing the measure, without either inquiring or reflecting.

There are reasons to be given in support of Independence, which men should rather privately think of, than be publicly told of. We ought not now to be debating whether we shall be independent or not, but, anxious to accomplish it on a firm, secure, and honorable basis, and uneasy rather that it is not yet began upon.

Every day convinces us of its necessity. Even the tories (if such beings yet remain among us) should, of all men, be the most solicitous to promote it; for, as the appointment of committees at first, protected them from popular rage, so, a wise and well established form of government, will be the only certain means of continuing it securely to them. Wherefore, if they have not virtue enough to be Whigs, they ought to have prudence enough to wish for independence.

In short, independence is the only bond that can tie and keep us together.

We shall then see our object, and our ears will be legally shut against the schemes of an intriguing, as well as a cruel enemy. We shall then too, be on a proper footing, to treat with Britain; for there is reason to conclude, that the pride of that court, will be less hurt by treating with the American states for terms of peace, than with those, whom she denominates, "rebellious subjects," for terms of accommodation.

It is our delaying it that encourages her to hope for conquest, and our backwardness tends only to prolong the war. As we have, without any good effect therefrom, withheld our trade to obtain a redress of our grievances, let us now try the alternative, by independently redressing them ourselves, and then offering to open the trade. The mercantile and reasonable part of England will be still with us; because, peace with trade, is preferable to war without it. And if this offer be not accepted, other courts may be applied to.

On these grounds I rest the matter.

And as no offer hath yet been made to refute the doctrine contained in the former editions of this pamphlet, it is a negative proof, that either the doctrine cannot be refuted, or, that the party in favor of it are too numerous to be opposed.

Wherefore, instead of gazing at each other with suspicious or doubtful curiosity, let each of us, hold out to his neighbor the hearty hand of friendship, and unite in drawing a line, which, like an act of oblivion, shall bury in forgetfulness every former dissention. Let the names of Whig and Tory be extinct; and let none other be heard among us, than those of a good citizen, an open and resolute friend, and a virtuous supporter of the RIGHTS of MANKIND and of the FREE AND INDEPENDENT STATES OF AMERICA.
EPISTLE TO QUAKERS

To the Representatives of the Religious Society of the People called Quakers, or to so many of them as were concerned in publishing a late piece, entitled "THE ANCIENT TESTIMONY and PRINCIPLES of the people called QUAKERS renewed with respect to the KING and GOVERNMENT, and Touching the COMMOTIONS now prevailing in these and other parts of AMERICA, addressed to the PEOPLE IN GENERAL."

THE writer of this is one of those few, who never dishonors religion either by ridiculing, or cavilling at any denomination whatsoever. To God, and not to man, are all men accountable on the score of religion. Wherefore, this epistle is not so properly addressed to you as a religious, but as a political body, dabbling in matters, which the professed quietude of your Principles instruct you not to meddle with.

As you have, without a proper authority for so doing, put yourselves in the place of the whole body of the Quakers, so, the writer of this, in order to be on an equal rank with yourselves, is under the necessity, of putting himself in the place of all those who approve the very writings and principles, against which your testimony is directed: And he hath chosen their singular situation, in order that you might discover in him, that presumption of character which you cannot see in yourselves. For neither he nor you have any claim or title to Political Representation.

When men have departed from the right way, it is no wonder that they stumble and fall.

And it is evident from the manner in which ye have managed your testimony, that politics, (as a religious body of men) is not your proper walk; for however well adapted it might appear to you, it is, nevertheless, a jumble of good and bad put unwisely together, and the conclusion drawn therefrom, both unnatural and unjust.

The two first pages, (and the whole doth not make four) we give you credit for, and expect the same civility from you, because the love and desire of peace is not confined to Quakerism, it is the natural, as well as the religious wish of all denominations of men.

And on this ground, as men laboring to establish an Independent Constitution of our own, do we exceed all others in our hope, end, and aim. Our plan is peace for ever.

We are tired of contention with Britain, and can see no real end to it but in a final separation. We act consistently, because for the sake of introducing an endless and uninterrupted peace, do we bear the evils and burdens of the present day. We are endeavoring, and will steadily continue to endeavor, to separate and dissolve a connection which hath already filled our land with blood; and which, while the name of it remains, will be the fatal cause of future mischiefs to both countries.

We fight neither for revenge nor conquest; neither from pride nor passion; we are not insulting the world with our fleets and armies, nor ravaging the globe for plunder. Beneath the shade of our own vines are we attacked; in our own houses, and on our own lands, is the violence committed against us.

We view our enemies in the characters of highwaymen and housebreakers, and having no defence for ourselves in the civil law; are obliged to punish them by the military one, and apply the sword, in the very case, where you have before now, applied the halter. Perhaps we feel for the ruined and insulted sufferers in all and every part of the continent, and with a degree of tenderness which hath not yet made its way into some of your bosoms. But be ye sure that ye mistake not the cause and ground of your Testimony. Call not coldness of soul, religion; nor put the bigot in the place of the Christian.

O ye partial ministers of your own acknowledged principles! If the bearing arms be sinful, the first going to war must be more so, by all the difference between wilful attack and unavoidable defence.

Wherefore, if ye really preach from conscience, and mean not to make a political hobby-horse of your religion, convince the world thereof, by proclaiming your doctrine to our enemies, for they likewise bear ARMS. Give us proof of your sincerity by publishing it at St. James's, to the commanders in chief at Boston, to the admirals and captains who are practically ravaging our coasts, and to all the murdering miscreants who are acting in authority under HIM whom ye profess to serve.

Had ye the honest soul of Barclay* ye would preach repentance to your king; Ye would tell the royal tyrant of his sins, and warn him of eternal ruin. Ye would not spend your partial invectives against the injured and the insulted only, but like faithful ministers, would cry aloud and spare none. Say not that ye are persecuted, neither endeavor to make us the authors of that reproach, which, ye are bringing upon yourselves; for we testify unto all men, that we do not complain against you because ye are Quakers, but because ye pretend to be and are NOT Quakers.

*"Thou hast tasted of prosperity and adversity; thou knowest what it is to be banished thy native country, to be overruled as well as to rule, and set upon the throne; and being oppressed thou hast reason to know now hateful the oppressor is both to God and man. If after all these warnings and advertisements, thou dost not turn unto the Lord with all thy heart, but forget him who remembered thee in thy

distress, and give up thyself to follow lust and vanity, surely great will be thy condemnation. Against which snare, as well as the temptation of those who may or do feed thee, and prompt thee to evil, the most excellent and prevalent remedy will be, to apply thyself to that light of Christ which shineth in thy conscience and which neither can, nor will flatter thee, nor suffer thee to be at ease in thy sins."- Barclay's Address to Charles II.

Alas! it seems by the particular tendency of some part of your Testimony, and other parts of your conduct, as if all sin was reduced to, and comprehended in the act of bearing arms, and that by the people only. Ye appear to us, to have mistaken party for conscience, because the general tenor of your actions wants uniformity: And it is exceedingly difficult to us to give credit to many of your pretended scruples; because we see them made by the same men, who, in the very instant that they are exclaiming against the mammon of this world, are nevertheless, hunting after it with a step as steady as Time, and an appetite as keen as Death.

The quotation which ye have made from Proverbs, in the third page of your testimony, that, "when a man's ways please the Lord, he maketh even his enemies to be at peace with him;" is very unwisely chosen on your part; because it amounts to a proof, that the king's ways (whom ye are so desirous of supporting) do not please the Lord, otherwise, his reign would be in peace.

I now proceed to the latter part of your testimony, and that, for which all the foregoing seems only an introduction, viz:

"It hath ever been our judgment and principle, since we were called to profess the light of Christ Jesus, manifested in our consciences unto this day, that the setting up and putting down kings and governments, is God's peculiar prerogative; for causes best known to himself: And that it is not our business to have any hand or contrivance therein; nor to be busy-bodies above our station, much less to plot and contrive the ruin, or overturn any of them, but to pray for the king, and safety of our nation, and good of all men: that we may live a peaceable and quiet life, in all goodliness and honesty; under the government which God is pleased to set over us."

If these are really your principles why do ye not abide by them? Why do ye not leave that, which ye call God's work, to be managed by himself? These very principles instruct you to wait with patience and humility, for the event of all public measures, and to receive that event as the divine will towards you. Wherefore, what occasion is there for your political Testimony if you fully believe what it contains? And the very publishing it proves, that either, ye do not believe what ye profess, or have not virtue enough to practice what ye believe.

The principles of Quakerism have a direct tendency to make a man the quiet and inoffensive subject of any, and every government which is set over him. And if the setting up and putting down of kings and governments is God's peculiar prerogative, he most certainly will not be robbed thereof by us; wherefore, the principle itself leads you to approve of every thing, which ever happened, or may happen to kings as being his work.

Oliver Cromwell thanks you. Charles, then, died not by the hands of man; and should the present proud imitator of him, come to the same untimely end, the writers and publishers of the Testimony, are bound by the doctrine it contains, to applaud the fact. Kings are not taken away by miracles, neither are changes in governments brought about by any other means than such as are common and human; and such as we are now using. Even the dispersing of the Jews, though foretold by our Savior, was effected by arms.

Wherefore, as ye refuse to be the means on one side, ye ought not to be meddlers on the other; but to wait the issue in silence; and unless you can produce divine authority, to prove, that the Almighty who hath created and placed this new world, at the greatest distance it could possibly stand, east and west, from every part of the old, doth, nevertheless, disapprove of its being independent of the corrupt and abandoned court of Britain; unless I say, ye can show this, how can ye, on the ground of your principles, justify the exciting and stirring up of the people "firmly to unite in the abhorrence of all such writings, and measures, as evidence a desire and design to break off the happy connection we have hitherto enjoyed, with the kingdom of Great Britain, and our just and necessary subordination to the king, and those who are lawfully placed in authority under him."

What a slap in the face is here! the men, who, in the very paragraph before, have quietly and passively resigned up the ordering, altering, and disposal of kings and governments, into the hands of God, are now recalling their principles, and putting in for a share of the business. Is it possible, that the conclusion, which is here justly quoted, can any ways follow from the doctrine laid down? The inconsistency is too glaring not to be seen; the absurdity too great not to be laughed at; and such as could only have been made by those, whose understandings were darkened by the narrow and crabby spirit of a despairing political party; for ye are not to be considered as the whole body of the Quakers but only as a factional and fractional part thereof.

Here ends the examination of your testimony; (which I call upon no man to abhor, as ye have done, but only to read and judge of fairly;) to which I subjoin the following remark; "That the setting up and putting down of kings," most certainly mean, the making him a king, who is yet not so, and the making him no king who is already one. And pray what hath this to do in the present case? We neither mean to set up nor to put down, neither to make nor to unmake, but to have nothing to do with them. Wherefore your testimony in whatever light it is viewed serves only to dishonor your judgment, and for many other reasons had better have been let alone than published.

First. Because it tends to the decrease and reproach of religion whatever, and is of the utmost danger to society, to make it a party in political disputes.

Secondly. Because it exhibits a body of men, numbers of whom disavow the publishing political testimonies, as being concerned therein and approvers thereof.

Thirdly. Because it hath a tendency to undo that continental harmony and friendship which yourselves by your late liberal and charitable donations hath lent a hand to establish; and the preservation of which, is of the utmost consequence to us all.

And here, without anger or resentment I bid you farewell. Sincerely wishing, that as men and Christians, ye may always fully and uninterruptedly enjoy every civil and religious right; and be, in your turn, the means of securing it to others; but that the example which ye have unwisely set, of mingling religion with politics, may be disavowed and reprobated by every inhabitant of America.

-THE END-

Source: Common Sense, by Thomas Paine, printed by W. and T. Bradford, Philadelphia, 1791.

The Fresh Start

Politics of Prosperity, Part II, Common Sense
by Anonymous
13 August 2013
Las Vegas, Nevada, USA

To contact the publisher:

usnvrepcan@gmail.com

Thanks for sharing this with people who care about America now and for our future...

www.ingramcontent.com/pod-product-compliance
Lightning Source LLC
Chambersburg PA
CBHW030922180526
45163CB00002B/438
9781492134527